Stirring It Up!

by Don Curto

With selections by
Patricia J. Tikkanen

Stirring It Up!
by Don Curto

With selections by
Patricia J. Tikkanen

Cover photo of Don Curto by Tom Buchkoe
Cover design by Kathy Jeske
kj graphics, Marquette, Michigan

Edited by Erin Elliott and Pat Ryan O'Day

Copyright 2002
Don Curto

Published by
Marquette Monthly
Thumbs Up Publishing
Marquette, Michigan

Publishing coordination by
Globe Printing, Inc.
Ishpeming, Michigan

Printed by Sheridan Books, Ann Arbor, Michigan

ISBN 0-9724913-0-9

November 2002

No portion of this book may be reproduced, reprinted or otherwise copied for distribution purposes without express written permission of the author and publisher.

Contents

Foreword   Tom Baldini   *vii*

Introduction   *ix*

A last look at the old
"Pere Marquette Inn"   15

What makes a good restaurant?   21

Brioche again?   *Patricia J. Tikkanen*   25

A is for Asparagus   29

The vegetables of Rome   35

The good egg returns   *Patricia J. Tikkanen*   41

There's something about spring   49

Bread: Its mystery & fascination   55

Bread: Forgotten art form?   59

Soup and bread   63

Summerthyme   *Patricia J. Tikkanen*   69

Potluck   *Patricia J. Tikkanen*   75

To shake or not to shake   83

Snowed in *Patricia J. Tikkanen*	87
In the olden days	95
My father and food	103
Finland, food and I	109
From the present to the past—and back again	115
An early spring in Italy	121
Love and passion in Rome, etc.	127
A love affair continued...three guys go to Italy	131
Meanderings far away	141
A working journey...and a sentimental one	147
A spicy love affair	153
Rituals of spring *with Patricia J. Tikkanen*	159
About smuggling, a Cardinal and the Vatican	167
Lessons learned in a berry patch *Patricia J. Tikkanen*	173
On being an almost purist	181
The joy of food	187

The perfect day	195
Life's riches	201
About manners, food, ruins and rejuvenation	207
It was a pretty slow millenium, but a damn fast century	213
On being an American citizen	221
The greatest generations	227
At the end, a lethal injection	229
Recipe index	*236*

Foreword
Tom Baldini

Having an interest in the qualities of good food and a belief in a certain philosophy of government are not that dissimilar—they both require passion, commitment, some inflexibility, strongly held opinions, and a willingness if not a desire to express those strongly held opinions to others.

Don Curto possesses these passions for food and politics. His long career has been crisscrossed by times of writing for newspapers, magazines or other publications expressing opinions or reporting the news. Other times he has ventured into the world of providing food to appreciative patrons. Both of these passions have permitted Don to express his opinion in either words or presentations on plates.

Don loves good food; preparing it, serving it to friends and talking about its aroma, sensation to the palate, texture and flavors, exchanging recipes and holding firm opinions about what is quality and what isn't quality food. If pressed, he will have an explanation of why something is great, good and passable, or not to be tried again. Don will not hesitate, even if not asked, to tell you what he thinks of what he sampled in on some recent visit to a restaurant or some new recipe.

Don is person of strong convictions. These strongly held beliefs are not confined to just food. Don has passionately held views about the role of government in the life of its citizens. He has a passion for the First Amendment and the rights of free speech and the free press—probably spawned from his work as a reporter and writer. He's a believer in the rights of the individual and the need to keep government in check. These long held political views have begun to appear with more frequency in his writings. His belief in the significance and importance of the individual and individual judgment and his desire to impose a standard (his!) on what is or isn't an excellent meal sometimes presents contradictions as he usurps that freedom of judgment of other individuals with his firm beliefs. That has not deterred Don, however. He knows what he believes and what he likes and he will probably let you know.

This publication of articles will satisfy those who have an appetite for food and politics. The articles are not for those with bland taste. They are heavily seasoned for the discriminating palate.

Introduction

I can best begin describing how I feel about food by relating how I feel about music. I like most jazz, classical and Italian opera, (a long dormant interest renewed by opera expert Pat Mayer) about in that order. I can, however, listen to and enjoy most music if the performers are good. So much of today's modern music consists mostly of high volume and lyrics with one or two words. There is little modern "music" that I enjoy. I do not consider "rap" to be acceptable music any more than I consider most "fast food," especially so-called "fast food Italian" to be acceptable food. (And a pox on the Chinese food "buffet.") One might as well eat margarine as eat that stuff. Some things are truly edible food products and some are not.

I have been called a "food snob" and depending upon who is making the charge, I don't find that too hard to live with. The charge usually means that I am very particular. That is correct. I like real people and real food. For over thirteen years my columns have been concerned with real food and real people and real issues. In this time I have only missed one month and this was when I thought that recovering from a replaced knee was easier than it in fact was. I wrote one column in a computer room atop the Hotel Continental which sits close by one end of the famed Ponte Vecchio in Florence, Italy. The management there trusted me with their business computer. A keyboard is a keyboard, of course, but all the instructions were in Italian. I managed to avoid destroying all their programs and sent the story directly to *MM*. It was the most beautiful setting for writing a story. The view to the west over Florence and the Arno River was magnificent with the sun setting and turning all the old buildings a soft gold.

In these thirteen years I have had a lot of help and encouragement from many people...including readers who contact me with comments. My first great helper was Mary Kinnunen, the founder of *MM* who said when I told her that her food columns were weak, "So, you're so smart, you try one." I did and it has been fun.

Pat Ryan O'Day, who has been the publisher of *MM* for over ten years has granted me more freedom than most writers ever hope for. We talk and we consult, but my freedom to write as I think necessary never has been restricted. One is lucky to get such a courageous publisher.

My wife, Pat, who has put up with a lot of complaining and some dietary excesses is represented here with a number of her own writings which only give a hint of just how good a writer she is.

Over the years of these columns the "Garden Club" has been a source of advice, fact gathering, complaints, insults to the writer of the columns but great support when required. Original Club members (Tom Baldini, Howard Cohodas, Judd Spray, Gary Walker and I) first met at the Vierling Restaurant for lunch on Fridays. We later moved to the N.Y. Deli when that opened. When I was thinking about starting the Deli, I remember asking what they thought of including chopped chicken livers and Matzo Ball soup on the menu. The uniform answer was "forget it." So how come we make chopped livers almost every other day and Matzo Ball Soup is one of the biggest sellers?

Judd Spray is the owner (the only one I know) of all the volumes

Stirring It Up!

of *The Oxford English Dictionary* and with that and his skill in other areas he is a wonderful fact checker and relentless critic (usually right) when permitted. The Garden Club, with looser membership requirements, still meets. And it still criticizes.

I don't want to skip my partner and chef, John Godo, who has taken on much of what I formerly did to give me time to write; he is my recipe tester, usually improving on the original.

There are many others who have helped me, given me ideas, and edited parts of my writing. Erin Elliott, a wonderfully capable recent Northern Michigan University English graduate, has been the editor for this volume. The book's appearance and accuracy has been her responsibility and the fun of working with her has been my reward. The cover was conceived and created by that talented artist, Kathy Jeske, who does such good work on *MM* designs.

As helpful as these people have been, they are relative newcomers to my life.

Two friends of almost thirty years standing have been my sources of information, education, and yes, inspiration.

My best teacher, operating from a lifetime of food experience and knowledge has been Ted Bogdan. Ted was for a long time a professor in NMU's prestigious foods program. He has acolytes around the world. There isn't a lot that he doesn't know about restaurant foods and he has always been willing to share with those of us with less knowledge. He's been my encyclopedia.

My best critic, by far, and collector of recipes, food information and interesting peripheral stuff has been Howard Cohodas. It is a rare day that he doesn't give me information gleaned by prodigious scouring of publications that I might never see. For a man who doesn't cook much personally, he has an unerring taste for quality and an uncanny ability to detect the phony, in food, in presentation, in service—and in people. He has never refrained from pointing out errors and ways that I could do better. I have in the short term *mostly* appreciated this...and in the long term, *always* appreciated the help.

DON CURTO

This book is thus dedicated to Ted Bogdan, my teacher and to Howard Cohodas, my critic, who in doing this tough job has also been a teacher. I hope it is worth it to them.

A last look at the old "Pere Marquette Inn"

There really is nothing architecturally elegant about this place, and certainly the furnishings were not chosen and coordinated by any interior decorator. The antique waiting bench along the right wall and the line of large, fully useful coat hooks on the left wall give this entrance way somewhat the look of a doctor's office, albeit an old fashioned one. But it has a feeling that goes beyond the shape and decoration. It's comfortable; it's appropriate.

Any ideas of antique are dispelled immediately by the hostess, a charming young person named Susan, uniformed in an engagingly appropriate dark skirt and white blouse, with high collar, set off by a string of dark green beads. Noting that there are only two of us in the party, she refrains from making the unnecessary query: "Are there only two in your party?" so often asked by a poorly trained hostess. With menus under her arm and a pleasingly quick walk, she leads us to a table near the window overlooking the lake and part of town, now lighted at evening.

She seats my wife, gives us menus, notes that we have water and informs us that Geri will be our waitress. She inquires if we wish to place a cocktail order and then departs to pick up the next waiting party. Not once did I have the feeling that she was rushed to get back to the other part of the job.

Like the entrance way, the dining room is plain, as you probably know, but is well furnished for the purpose of feeding customers in relative comfort, without making the place look like a greenhouse or antique parlor of London's glory days. Everything here is directed to the reason that one visits—to eat food. There are only twenty tables, with plenty of space around them. All the tables along the front windows, with the best view, are for two persons, so no one sits with their back to the window.

For dinner, the place setting is on white tablecloths with large white cotton napkins, a small arrangement of real flowers in the center of the table, and particularly high grade stainless flatware, as evidenced by the heavy and well balanced knives and forks. Glassware is not crystal, of course, but it is glass and the quality seems good. The whole table is good enough to say "quality" but not so overdone and heavy as to draw attention to itself and frighten us off. I get the feeling that my food is going to be presented as nicely.

Geri comes, and does all the things that a well trained waitress is supposed to do. The dining room is very busy and so is Geri, but she takes time to tell us the specials for the evening, ask for any special needs and says she'll return. The requested coffee comes and we decide on our order.

First, we share a plate of poached whitefish pieces which have been cooked in white wine and are served beautifully on a plate barely covered with green onion sauce. A fresh grinding of pepper on top completes the picture. Three small pieces each is enough appetizer.

We both order a cup of the spinach soup and it comes, thick with chopped fresh spinach in a very rich chicken broth, just barely flavored with nutmeg and topped with pieces of feta cheese. What a nice touch. (Especially noteworthy is the absence of soda crackers

Stirring It Up!

in the armor-like cellophane.)

I notice that the relatively new sound-absorbing ceiling tiles really seem to cut the decibel level—the last time I was here, the noise was bothersome.

We choose different salads: I love mushrooms, so I get the mushroom, blue cheese and walnut salad; Pat orders the spinach with bacon and apples. The mushroom salad is made up of an appropriate pile of slightly cooked and marinated sliced large mushrooms, chunks of spicy blue cheese and crunchy toasted walnuts for garnish. The spinach salad consists of obviously fresh spinach, torn into bite-size pieces, mixed with slices of Delicious apples, toasted almonds and crumbled crisp bacon. A light vinaigrette adds the final touch.

The crackly crisp-crusted fresh Italian bread with unsalted butter caps this course with real class. It is a pleasure to bite into bread made by a baker who loves his product and understands how despicable are long loaves of floppy bread wrapped in plastic.

The entree special for the night is a different mix of beef and seafood, sort of a new "surf & turf," though, thank God, the term is never mentioned. The accompanying starch is a totally different pasta mix.

I first had the pasta dish back in '83 at another area restaurant that specialized in unusual Friday night dinners—fettucini with walnut sauce, an amazingly fine dish from Argentina, which is really not known for its Italian food. Our waitress knows enough about the kitchen to tell us that the noodles are first cooked, then quickly sauced with a mixture of sour cream and whole cream and kept warm. Melted butter, flavored with garlic, is quickly heated, then chopped walnuts, Parmesan cheese and some rich chicken broth are added. This is poured over the noodles, tossed and served as an accompaniment.

The meat/seafood combination is made up of fairly thin slices of beef filet, sauteed in butter and oil, just until brown and warm and three very large peeled shrimp, cooked in garlic butter, placed artistically atop the filets. The noodles are served on the same plate, with a green garnish of fresh rosemary sprigs between the items.

It would be hard to think of a better combination of foods for a simple, Saturday night dinner. The beef and shrimp make a wonderful taste pair and the walnut and noodles add a special crunchiness.

For dessert we both have a dish that is so good, so simple and so well liked by almost everyone who ever tries it that I find it hard to understand why almost every restaurant doesn't have it on its menu—and as a bonus, it is a highly profitable menu item. You might hear of this dessert as "Creme Caramel," which is French for "custard with caramel sauce." It consists of caramelized sugar and a plain custard of eggs, sugar and milk or cream, with a touch of vanilla extract. Material cost for a five-ounce serving is less than twenty-five cents and it sells for anywhere from $1.25 to $3.25 depending on the restaurant, and whether it is called creme caramel, or custard with caramel. The two big factors that can spoil this dish are slightly burning the caramel and overcooking the custard. The Pere Marquette does neither.

Coffee was hot and rich, deep with flavor. Clearly, management had learned "the coffee lesson"—the very finest coffee obtainable is the biggest bargain in the restaurant business. Even when using all Columbian coffee, one of the most expensive, a brewed cup costs about three cents. Except for lack of knowledge or bad taste, or both, there is no reason for anyone to use junk coffee.

John Frost, the food and beverage manager, sat with us after dinner and talked about the problems in running this place. Management and staff, he says, are the biggest problems; good food items are obtainable easily these days from major food distributors, supplemented when necessary by local shopping and some farm visits for speciality items. Because of great progress in the past ten years, even as remote an area (from a transportation perspective) as Marquette County now has a fine variety of restaurant foods available readily from both wholesale and retail outlets.

Stirring It Up!

Frost noted that the restaurant business is one of the last major operations which require neither licensing nor certification for employees. Anyone can work in a kitchen and beyond management's requirements, there are none imposed by government which cannot be bypassed easily. He pointed out that one cannot get a dead body ready for burial unless a state licensed person does the work, nor can one get a hair cut by an unlicensed barber, but we put food in our mouths prepared by people we often know nothing about; and the changeover is so frequent in some food establishments, that sometimes even management know little about the employee, who, figuratively, puts their fingers in our mouths.

John holds "school" for kitchen and dining room help at least monthly and requires all kitchen employees, regardless of duty, to pass the county health department sanitation tests and be certified.

He also noted that many small restaurant management people are still in the pencil and paper days in an already established computer age. The Pere Marquette, he said, is computerized down to its recipe cost controls, with everything standardized as much as possible, so that management is never at the mercy of a single cook who may walk off with a favorite recipe. Making the standard routine, John notes, lets him and his cooks spend more time working on special, creative dishes—which, if they are successful with the public, become "standard" too.

Well, his ideas must work, because this certainly is one of the best meals we have had in a very long time in this area—yet there was nothing complex about it. All preparations were simple and it is little wonder that the Pere Marquette is without peer.

I highly recommend this place and though directions to reach it remain somewhat murky, I have great hopes that in the future, the Pere Marquette, more or less, will be everywhere in our area. Its principles and methods are simple and here for everyone to use.

Bon appetit!, which, freely translated from the French, means "Boy, am I hungry!"

—March 1992

Stirring It Up!

What makes a good restaurant?

This month's piece looks at the restaurant business from a different perspective: how do we judge them? A recent study published in a number of trade journals reported that forty-three cents of each dollar Americans spent on food in 1991 was spent in restaurants. That's a lot of money to be subject to the whims, dreams and standards (both good and bad) of restaurant owners, many of whom are untrained in the food business.

Do we get our money's worth? How will we know if we do? What are some standards to look for? When I review a restaurant, I use the following guidelines when determining what I think of the place.

First I look for *pleasant service* by trained people—waiters and waitresses who have been around long enough to know the menu and to know the regular customers—I am wary of a place where employee turnover is high. I also am cautious in a place where it is apparent that the manager has told the help that "the customer is always right." No professional I ever met really believes that. The customer is not always right; but the customer is always human and should be treated so, even if he or she has to be gently denied some impossible request.

Food feeds the body, but *surroundings and decoration* feed the spirit. "Busy" decoration, walls plastered with discordant "junk" and inappropriate decor vex the spirit and disturb digestion.

I now come to the heart of the matter, *food and its preparation.*

First, three of my pet peeves. I don't think that in order to qualify as a good restaurant, a place must serve what has become known as "gourmet cooking." There are plenty of glitzy French, continental and Italian places around the country that promise the stars (and charge accordingly), but never fulfill the promise.

On the other hand, there's this myth about truck stops. According to legend, the decor is crude and the cook and proprietor need a shave, but the food is great—especially the coffee. I have stopped at some of these truck stops and my experience has been that most are popular truck stops because: 1) the parking lot is big enough to park the big rigs; 2) prices are low; 3) they are open twenty-four hours; and 4) waitresses are quick witted enough to add some spice to a long, dull trip. Quality of food has little to do with their popularity.

My experience also has taught me to avoid places that advertise "home cooking" or "just like mother made." Most home cooking is nowhere near as good as a decent restaurant and it has a lot less variety. My mother was a pretty good mother, as mothers go, but I know that the cooks where I eat are better than my mother was; she was half Irish, half French Canadian, and an outstanding example of these two disparate food cultures in conflict.

So what do I want restaurant food to be? Everything about a restaurant makes a promise to a customer which is fulfilled (or not) in its food and how it is presented. It starts with the menu, for it is the menu that tells the most important part of a restaurant's story and it is the menu that makes the biggest promises.

We all know the aphorism, "Be careful what you pray for, you

Stirring It Up!

may get it." There is another that applies to restaurant owners: "Be wary of what you offer, you may have to deliver." Michigan, I'm led to believe, has a "truth in menu" law, but I doubt it gets enforced frequently.

There are menus that directly note or imply that the orange juice is "fresh squeezed," when in fact it's made from frozen concentrate. Or, that the rolls are "homemade," when in fact they've only been reheated on site. Homemade chili is often packaged chili, more or less modified with additional meat, spices, etc. "Real mashed potatoes" that seem real because they have lumps in them may be dried potatoes, as those "lumps" are now available from suppliers.

In truth it should be pointed out that more often than not, pre-made foods are better looking, better prepared and better tasting than a lot of stuff made "from scratch." Still, restaurants should be honest.

In addition to a truthful menu, the food sent to the table should be well prepared and attractively garnished. "Well prepared" means such things as being cooked properly, being served at the right temperature and having the right "mix" for appearance, nutrition and taste.

On the down side of nouvelle and so-called healthy cuisine is the all-too-frequent error of making a plate of tasteless food look like a work of art. I also object to restaurants announcing that the kitchen cooks without salt and uses margarine instead of butter for my health. Please, don't watch my health for me, I'll take care of that. Besides, who said margarine is better for me than butter? And, with many foods, shaken-on salt does not take the place of cooked-in salt in enhancing food flavors. In short, food should taste good.

I also look for some imagination in food preparation—perhaps some use of seasonal foods or Lake Superior products. There aren't too many compelling reasons to use frozen fish in place of white-fish or trout, except that the wholesale purveyors often can deliver ocean fish more easily (and cheaply) than the Lake Superior fish. But this is not always the case. Frequently it is only because it is easier to have a product delivered than to go out and get it.

Imagination also includes garnish—curly parsley is *not* the only green garnish.

Finally, I look to see if the decor, the menu and the service match. Am I presented with a fine menu, pleasant service and ugly decor, or some other combination of failures?

It's difficult to go anywhere these days for an evening meal for two and spend less than fifteen dollars—it is frequently much more than this. Often, meal costs are driven up, for instance, by the charges for a cup of coffee—sixty cents to one dollar. (I use $7.90 per pound coffee at home which works out to be just about five cents a cup. Restaurant coffee costs less than half of this. When is the last time you protested coffee prices?)

So, when you go out to eat, don't let restaurants promise you things that you know they can't deliver; and certainly complain when expectations aren't met. When we remain silent we permit the continuation of poor food, poor service, etc. The more grandiose the unfulfilled promise, the more barbed the criticism should be. Let places know what your expectations are. There may be only a few of us privileged enough to put our opinions in print, but anyone who eats out has the right, and maybe the obligation, to criticize when standards aren't met. It's your money.

—November 1992

Brioche again?

Patricia J. Tikkanen

Publisher's Note: Don Curto, the regular writer of Food and Other Important Things, *announced to me a few weeks ago that even columnists deserve an occasional vacation and he was taking his this issue. Fortunately, the following piece then appeared mysteriously on his desk.*

My husband is well known in our community as a chef. He has owned a popular restaurant, taught culinary arts at the local university, writes a column on food for the local monthly magazine and has his own cooking show on television. No one actually has organized a fan club and I wouldn't describe his admirers as "groupies," but it is seldom that we are out anywhere that someone doesn't come up to comment about a recently demonstrated recipe, ask a question about cooking or just say that they enjoyed a recent show or article.

When I am introduced, the question I get asked, especially from other women, is, "Does he *really* do the cooking at home?" (In a sense this is an indication of the general level of liberation in our society since I really can't imagine someone turning to Mr. Childs and asking, "Now, does Julia *really* cook your dinner?") I always answer honestly that he does do all of the cooking and yes, I know I'm a lucky woman.

And I am...mostly. Now I realize that I'm probably not going to get a lot of sympathy from a woman whose husband's notion of competent cooking is remembering to take the package of gizzards out of the chicken before putting the bird in the oven. Spouses of either sex who have eaten "hamburger glop" once too often or where "home-cooked" has come to mean any meal served on the family's own china regardless of the cartons it came out of, also may be a mite dubious. Still, before you simply label me as a self-pitying whiner, let me have my say.

First, even the best chef has to practice to perfect his technique. This means that dietary selections can be somewhat limited from week to week. For example, a few years ago, my husband was preparing to teach a class on brioche, which he described as "the most elegant of all the yeast bread doughs, rich in butter and eggs." The first week brioche shaped into various sized loaves and rolls accompanied every meal. The second week brioche became the entree—chicken in brioche, brioche stuffed with ground beef, steak wrapped in brioche, and so on. The third week the meal became brioche—sausages in brioche for an appetizer, pizza made with brioche for the entree and brioche bread pudding for dessert. It's one meal I will never forget.

Next, it must be understood that it is never enough for the resident chef to just have his food eaten. Food in general is important and *this* food is critically important. It requires thoughtful comment. Now, if the meal is a household standby (say, stracciatella soup, a spinach frittata, a salad of romaine lettuce with gorgonzola dressing, and foccacia with garlic cloves) simple laudatory remarks may suffice. Even under these conditions, however, it is important to recognize each dish and ideally this should be done within the first two-and-a-half minutes of beginning to eat. For example, if the above meal was on our table and I had commented on the soup,

Stirring It Up!

"My favorite," the frittata, "superb," and the salad, "refreshing," my husband's next comment would likely be, "So, you don't like the bread tonight?"

When the dish is new and still being perfected by the chef, much more is required—informed, thoughtful comment. This requires that the non-chef spouse develop a certain amount of vocabulary about the food as well as a discerning palate. Recently my husband has developed a new cinnamon roll for an out-of-town restaurant where he is serving as a consultant. My comment after the fifteenth roll of the week illustrates my advancement to a new level of proficiency. "Now this is getting good. The dough tastes like a brioche and the hint of rum in the filling is inspired. I would suggest just a little less nutmeg in relationship to the cinnamon and a little more apple puree." Not bad for a woman who still likes soup out of red and white cans.

This ability for informed, thoughtful commentary can be useful if the chef is working on a dish that really is appreciated by the commentator. The trick here is to take your time in declaring the dish "Perfect!" We frequently travel to a community where there is an Italian restaurant that features a slow-baked herbed chicken. I love this chicken. To please me my husband decided to perfect the recipe and technique at home. After a few attempts he has, but will I acknowledge this? Of course not. If I did, he would file the recipe somewhere and go on to another challenge. And so I comment, "Very good, but I think there is still a bit too much oregano in the seasoning and the skin could be just a bit crispier."

Up until now I've probably given the impression that all mandatory taste tests are done in the context of a meal. In fact, the non-chef may be summoned at any time for duties which can involve restrained, informed, thoughtful commentary. Such was the case when my husband was preparing for a television show featuring vegetables. I had just finished dressing for work when I heard him call, "Come down for a real taste treat." When I joined him in our kitchen he motioned me to the table, "Just try that!"

I moved to the table and looked down at a bowl of...cucumber soup. The creamy broth was rich with butter and speckles of dill floated among the green pieces of cucumber. It was a moment requiring more love than culinary knowledge as I responded, "The colors are fantastic, but...is there any of that brioche left?"

• • •

Nearly Perfect Italian Roast Chicken for Two Not-So-Perfect People
Take the halves of a split small broiler chicken (buy them this way or cut them yourself), thoroughly wash in salted cold water and pat dry with paper towels. In a double thick grocery bag place a mixture as follows: 1 tablespoon each of dried thyme, oregano, marjoram, basil, rosemary and sage. Shake chicken well to heavily coat halves.

Place on a sheet pan and cook uncovered in a pre-heated 450 degree F. oven for twenty-five minutes. Reduce heat to 250 degrees F. and add one cup water to pan, cover chicken loosely with aluminum foil and cook for thirty minutes longer.

Remove foil, continue to cook for forty-five minutes longer.

Zucchini, yellow squash and fresh tomatoes go well with this. Or, cook rice or pasta and add it to the vegetables.

—September 1991

A is for Asparagus

As this is written in late May I happily report that Asparagus are being harvested in lower Michigan and that late yesterday I carried carefully a bag of them across the Bridge and that I just now have finished a good bunch of them, simmered shortly and simply in water in a saute pan, lightly brushed with melted butter, sprinkled with a bit of Parmesan cheese, salted gently, eaten in solitude using fingers as tongs and slurping with pleasure and having to listen to no well-meaning comments about a more gentlemanly way of eating Asparagus. There are, it is true, especially in public, other ways of eating these wonders, but none I think providing more pleasure.

When real local Asparagus come into my life I capitalize them as one of God's great gifts to both humans, and to my Black Labrador Kate who will eat them with me as she does the first tomatoes of the year and any ripe banana or flavorful apple at any time.

The Michigan Asparagus Advisory Board is very helpful with good information. Asparagus is a member of the Lily family and they grow from a "crown" that is planted about a foot deep in a sandy soil. After planting, the first harvesting takes about three years in order to give the roots a chance to develop a strong system. If well cared for, plantings will produce for about fifteen years! Under ideal conditions, plants can grow ten inches in a twenty-four-hour period and each crown will send spears up for about six to seven weeks during spring and early summer. Outdoor temperature determines how much time will be between each picking. Early in the season, there may be four to five days between pickings and as the days and nights get warmer, a particular field may have to be picked every twenty-four hours. Asparagus is loaded with nutrients for us. It is high in Folic Acid and is a good source of potassiuim, fiber, vitamin B6, vitamins A and C, and thiamin. Asparagus has no fat, no cholesterol and is low in sodium. This information should keep you away from the so-called health food shelves where you can spend your money on stuff you probably do not need.

As with much of the nation's yearly "vegetable menu," Asparagus are now available in stores every month, all year. They are grown in California, in Mexico, and other strange and mysterious places. Conglomerates put their colorful labels on them and mostly they are expensive, skinny and pretty and virtually tasteless. Pretty, tasteless, uninteresting, applies to too much of what we eat for lack of available "real" food. But that is the topic for a later column.

Not well known is the relationship of skinny stalks to thick stalks: experts declare that the larger the stalk diameter the better the quality. (Is there any chance that this could, too, apply to us humans?) The French say that thick stalks need to be peeled at the base in order that the whole stalk will cook uniformly. My experience is that this is true under two conditions: 1) if the stalk is not very fresh and 2) if the steaming method of cooking is used, espe-

Stirring It Up!

cially the one calling for tied stalks to be placed in a double boiler with the tops protruding from the water.

The Asparagus I got this week near Lansing included many very thick stalks, but they just had been picked in the nearby field. I only use one cooking method: put enough water in a large saute pan to cover whatever amount of *Asparagus* you will cook. Bring it to a boil, sprinkle lightly with salt, put in Asparagus, all as nearly same size as posible (you can, if you are so inclined, say a short prayer of appreciation). Drop water to barely simmer. Cook uncovered just until crisp/tender, about five minutes, sometimes less. Check them. Then drain, eat any way you wish. If they are fresh, peeling is unnecessary.

Asparagus is the kind of delicacy requiring little embellishment to get full appreciation of their elegance. Except for a Sunday brunch at home I prefer to eat the most simple recipe: cook the Asparagus, drain, place on a beautiful plate, pour a very small amount of melted butter over them, sprinkle very gently with Parmesan cheese, some black pepper and enjoy. Best if eaten with fingers.

There is a nice Sunday brunch plate, too. Cook Asparagus and place on beautiful plate, cook two fresh **eggs,** sunnyside up, place them carefully on top of the Asparagus with both green ends showing. Sprinkle eggs with Parmesan, salt and pepper. Enjoy.

There has to be a *pasta* dish with Asparagus, of course. I have seen many recipes using pasta with Asparagus, but the best taste combination, I think, is one using either shrimp or scallops, but not both at the same time. Let's use shrimp.

Cook a pound of fresh Asparagus, to just past totally raw—do not overcook for this recipe. Cool under running cold water, drain, cut into tips and pieces about an inch- or posssibly an inch-and-a quarter long. Set aside.

Peel about a pound of raw medium shrimp. Chop about one-half cup scallions, using mostly the green part. Prepare one-half cup chicken stock. Measure one-half cup unsalted butter. Cook one-half pound fettuccine, cooked, drained and set aside.

The rest is easy: melt the butter in a skillet, saute the shrimp until pink, beginning to brown, add chopped onion, now add Asparagus, stock, seasonings, fettuccine, stir and cook until warm. Serve in a large heated bowl. Garnish with lemon slices.

Now the only thing you have to do is hope that you can find some real Asparagus.

• • •

Eldorado of the North

In 1876 a Time Table Guide for the Marquette, Houghton and Ontonagon Railroad Company demonstrated that marketing skills and publicity writing were as good then as now, possibly even better. This railroad, which had its general offices in Marquette, served a small area, running from Marquette through Bancroft, Morgan, Eagle Mill, Negaunee, Ishpeming, Ontario Junction, Saginaw, Greenwood, Clarksburg, Humboldt, Republic, (via a short branch) Champion, Michigamme, Spurr, Sturgeon, Summit and L'Anse. (How many of these stops can you find today?) A short line ran from there to Ontonagon and another to Houghton. The railroad's connection to the outer, big world was through Ishpeming via the Chicago & Northwestern Railway to Chicago and then the world.

This was a real timetable, with train times for each point, a route map and some great advertising incorporated:

"Europeans," it said, "visiting America to attend the Centennial Exhibition should avail themselves of the reduction in R.R. and Steamboat fares during the summer months, to visit the Iron, Silver and Copper mines of the Lake Superior Region.

"Here is to be found the most extensive Iron and the most valuable Copper mines in the world. Names of Iron Mines and Furnaces with Location on M.H.&O.R.R.: In Marquette: Marquette and Pacific Furnace, Carp, Grace. In Bancroft: Bancroft. The Morgan in Morgan, in Negaunee: Rolling Mill Mine, McComber, Jackson. In Ishpeming: New York, Cleveland, Lake Superior Mine, Lake Angeline. In Saginaw: the Saginaw, Winthrop, Shenango; the Greenwood Furnace in Greenwood, the Michigan in Clarksburg

Stirring It Up!

and in Humboldt: Washington Mine, Edwards, Franklin, Hungerford. In Republic: Republic, Kloman, Peninsula, Metropolis, Erie, Cannon, Magnetic. The Keystone in Champion, the Michigamme and the Harney in Michgamme and the Spurr and Stewart in Spurr.

"Silver is being discovered of so great richness and in such quantities as to promise that in the future this region shall bear the title of Eldorado of the North.

"This country is covered with charming natural scenery, and your time can be constantly spent finding new objects of interest and scenes of beauty which will leave their impression on your memory forever. The sportsman will find deer, partridges and other wild game in abundance. For the angler there are speckled brook trout in all the streams in this section, and the lake trout will afford all the sport desired. The pure and bracing air of this region is unequaled in any other portion of the United States, the thermometer rarely rises beyond seventy or eighty degrees during the day, and blankets are indispensible during the night. The contrast in this respect between this section of the country and the hot and oppressive air of the Southern and Eastern States is most remarkable, and the change decidedly beneficial."

During this time my grandfather John Tobin was getting ready to court a rare beauty in Champion named Ida Beaudette. He won her, but my observation of them late in their lives is that he wished he hadn't. We never became the Eldorado of the North and by the time the extractors and the cutters finished their work a lot of our scenery took several generations to return.

But, it's pretty now.

—June 2001

The vegetables of Rome

Each year, when real tomatoes become extinct, along about the middle of October around here, I begin to slide into a "vegetable depression," which while initially relatively mild by mental health standards, begins a spiral toward severity when I realize that it will be eight or nine months yet before I am likely to see a truly edible tomato in the markets.

I still have about two dozen ripening tomatoes from our garden wrapped in newsprint; these will be ripe and eaten in a couple of weeks. I think that I have mentioned before in this space that my father was an accomplished "tomato person." For a number of years, his tomatoes regularly won prizes at the old Marquette County Fair and it was he who taught me about wrapping in newspaper. He staged the picking of his green tomatoes so that those least ripe would not mature under their newsprint coats until about the middle of December. Memory becomes inaccurate and untrustworthy I suppose, but I seem to recall that one year we had real tomatoes at Christmas.

From now until the late Spring of 1998, we face pale tomatoes—grown in Mexico, where pesticides still reportedly are permitted and where, alas, some of the fertilizer is suspect—or the pretty, bright red and expensive hydroponically grown tomato. This product looks good, but tastes exactly as though it were grown in liquid chemicals; it has little "body" and tends to become mush shortly after you spend your whole shopping budget on these red beauties.

You probably, by this time, are aware that suppliers' warehouses are stocked with green tomatoes. When ordered for delivery, cases are taken into ripening rooms where they are treated to an atmosphere of ethylene gas. Thus your "ripe" tomato, overnight, gets ready for its journey to you.

Unfortunately, despite all these complaints, I find it necessary to purchase these products. I lament that Ecclesiastes was wrong, everything, apparently, down not have its season. Oh, well.

• • •

So what is one to do for the unusual vegetable accompaniment to provide solace for the temporary loss of the lovely tomato? When in Rome, do as the Romans do, but when in the U.P. copy as much as possible, innovate and modify. I speak here of the wonderful vegetables of Rome, those roasted slices of eggplants, the various squashes, the peppers, etc. I am far from being a vegetarian, but the roasted vegetables offered at lunch in almost any trattoria in Rome could make one think seriously about not eating meat to make room for just one more bite of the vegetables.

And, fortunately, we do have available to us as winter approaches very good sweet peppers (green, red, yellow—though the latter two are very expensive). We still can get very nice small potatoes, excellent carrots, sweet onions, eggplant, zucchini and yellow squash. Most of these will be available all winter. Purchase a variety. Next, buy some really good olive oil being sure to get only extra virgin. Olive oil taste is important in this use.

Let's assume you get small potatoes, carrots, eggplant, onion, zucchini and yellow squash (the small are best). Boil the small

Stirring It Up!

An Italian market

potatoes and the peeled carrots. If the larger end of the carrots is thick, cut these in half so that cooking will be even, but keep carrot length about two and one-half or three inches. Cook until just barely done—do not overcook. Peel the eggplant and cut slices about a quarter inch thick. If the diameter of the slices is big, cut the slices in half. Peel the squashes, and cut into pieces about four inches long and then slice these into strips (the long dimension) and about a quarter-inch thick. Peel the onions, and prepare about three slices from the center of the onion, each about one-half inch thick.

Depending upon how well you and your guests like vegetables, allow three or four pieces of each vegetable for each. Set your oven temperature to 400 degrees F.

Now drain the potatoes and the carrots, cut potatoes in half, and arrange them along with the carrots on an oiled sheet pan(s). Place the slices of the other vegetables on the same pan until they are all spread out evenly, including the onion slices. Brush each piece, including the potatoes and the carrots, with olive oil. For a tasty variation, brush both the zucchini and the yellow squash with oil flavored with garlic. Bake at 400 degrees F. for about fifteen minutes, possibly less. The potatoes and carrots already are cooked and the onion should be crisp for eating, so the cooking time should be judged by the eggplant and the squashes. If you use any of the sweet peppers, cut them in half-inch strips and as they need no advance cooking, place them on the baking sheet and treat as the others with oil.

After baking, get your oven broiler ready. Remove the pan from the oven and again brush each piece liberally with the good olive oil. Place under the broiler until the vegetables are nicely browned. Be gentle.

If you are using two pans only one goes under the broiler. Since there is no need to eat these vegetables while they are hot, just set one pan aside while you do the other one. As a matter of taste, it is better to eat these after they have cooked a bit.

My friend and fellow cook Ted Bogdan says that these vegetables make a fine sandwich when they are cool. He notes that the current American fascination with grilling vegetables instead of the more careful preparation noted above produces tasteless food. Sometimes there is no quick way to good eating.

• • •

Make Your Own Bread
When testing the above procedure for this column I decided to also bake a loaf of bread so that the well prepared vegetables could be eaten with made-at-home bread. Making good bread is such a simple process that I wonder why we don't do it more often. Gathering ingredients and utensils (*mise en place)* takes about five minutes. Proofing the yeast and mixing with flour, etc. another fifteen minutes. Rising, except for preparing the bowl for the dough, while it takes an hour or so requires none of the baker's time. Go watch TV. Take a nap. This loaf is being prepared for sandwiches so it is to be baked in a bread loaf pan. Most times, a second rising after the initial one will produce a loaf of better taste, but if you don't have the time, a single rising is fine, too. After the loaf is formed and placed in the pan, there is another rise (to the top of the loaf pan) and then into the oven at 375 degrees F., until the bottom when tapped produces a hollow sound. Note that it is the bottom, not the top. If the loaf needs more baking, it does not

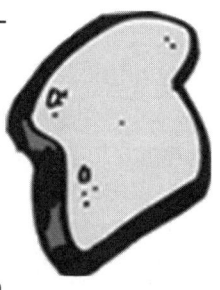

Stirring It Up!

have to be returned to the pan, but can continue baking on the baking sheet, or merely on the oven rack. Hands-on work here is less than thirty minutes.

The most basic bread is made with water, yeast, salt and flour. You can leave the salt out if you wish, as bakers do with a famous bread in Florence, Italy. The conversion of water, yeast and flour into a fine tasting bread is as near a miracle of food as I've seen.

Here's what you need:

1 C. water at 115 degrees F.
2 tsp. active dry yeast (2 tsp. is plenty—most recipes call for about twice the amount of yeast you need)
1 tsp. salt
2-1/2 to 3 C. flour

Add a little more flour and drop a whole egg in the mixing bowl to add some flavor and some tenderness to the loaf. You can add a tablespoon of olive oil also, or some butter. A fat added will produce a more tender loaf of bread.

• • •

Speaking of Fat...Be Careful
Margarine, that evil old culprit, is back in the news again. Trans fatty acids, substances prominent in so many of our processed and "fast" foods, margarines and some vegetable oils have been found in a new study of European women (reported in *The N.Y. Times* on Oct. 14) to increase by forty percent the chances for breast cancer. The study is reported to be relevant especially to American women because their intake of trans fatty acids is about double that of Europeans. Previous studies have linked these fats to an increased risk of heart disease. Trans fatty acids do not occur naturally, but are hydrogenated to form margarine and other solid vegetable oils which are not normally solid at room temperature. They also are added to some vegetable oils to prolong shelf life, although this fact

is not stated on the label.

It takes about two years on a good diet containing less of these fats to reduce the deposits in human body fat. Another argument for using olive oil whenever possible.

Regarding margarine, a product I heartily dislike: If margarine is good, in and of itself, why do they make it look like butter? Use butter, just don't use so much of it.

Well, that's probably enough trouble for one month.

—November 1997

The good egg returns
Patricia J. Tikkanen

When I was nine my family moved to live with my grandfather Tikkanen a few miles south of Calumet on the farm where my father had grown up. At the time my grandfather had a small flock of chickens housed in an old-fashioned chicken coop complete with multi-tiered nests in wooden crates and an outdoor fenced-in area where the hens could scratch around during the summer. My dad decided to expand this business and within a few years, we had flocks of up to 2,500 birds kept in neat rows of metal cages slanted so that the eggs would roll in a ledge for easy gathering. I, however, had little to do with that part of the business, for which I was glad. I had developed a bit of a phobia about chickens when gathering the eggs in that coop and one of the hens took exception to me taking away the product of her hard work. I still get uncomfortable walking through the poultry barns at the local fairs sure that those hens can just sense that I'm terrified of them.

Actually, if I were to ever place my experience with eggs on my resume I don't think it would be grandiose to list my title as the *director of marketing* with joint appointments in *packaging and quality assurance*. Of course at the time I mostly was referred to as the *egg girl*. Perhaps not a high status title but at the time one to which no shame was associated since this was before the reputation of eggs on the healthy food scale sunk almost as low as double fudge cheesecake and French-fried potatoes with gravy.

Practicing our skills in empathy, we need to consider what a blow this had to be to a food that at one time was considered almost essential to a well-balanced breakfast. And remember the boiled egg diet? (For those too young, this consisted of almost nothing but hard-boiled eggs and grapefruit for a week. I assume people really did lose weight doing this. I never had the discipline to make it more than a day and a half.)

Then a new word started to make its way into our language—*cholesterol*. Few of us probably ever really understood what this was but we did get the idea—it was bad and the foods that had "it" were bad for us. And eggs are high in cholesterol at over 200 milligrams in a large egg. (There is some debate here with the American Egg Board using the figure 213 milligrams of cholesterol in a large egg and other sources using a figure of 250 to 275. All cholesterol is found in the egg yolk.) At any rate, since the current U.S. Dietary Guideline is only 300 milligrams per day, one eggs gets us a long way toward that figure regardless of whose figures are used. And so whole eggs became almost a forbidden food and eating them a form of self-destruction. Needless to say the self-esteem of the poor defenseless egg was damaged as career options plummeted, unless you were willing to separate and join the egg-beaters' crowd.

Well, in case you haven't noticed, eggs now are fighting back with prime time television commercials, glossy print ads and several web pages exhorting their redemption. According to the egg

Stirring It Up!

"spin doctors" it seems that the word we should have been concerned about all these years was not so much cholesterol, but fat. (For details on the studies cited by the PR folks for eggs check out the web page of the American Egg Board [www.aeb.org/]. Note, however, that there still is a debate among nutrition experts about eggs as part of a healthy diet with some experts challenging the study results.) Eggs, while not exactly low fat at four and one-half grams in a large egg (my favorite cookies have five for every two cookies and my "diet" popcorn has eight) are fairly economic calorie-wise with only seventy in that same large size. Capitalizing on the fact that for this seventy calories they also provide a good dollop of protein, are rich in essential nutrients, relatively inexpensive and easy to prepare, the Egg Nutrition Council (web page: www.enc-online.org) uses the tag line, "Eggs: delicious, nutritious, affordable fast food." And, not to be outdone, the American Egg Board site plays a little jingle from time to time with the lyrics, "the incredible, edible egg!"

While you will have to make your own decision about what to make of this new twist on eggs I frankly am relieved as it has helped me deal with some long-term guilt as a health professional dedicated to helping folks change unhealthy behavior of all kinds. Now I finally can come out of the carton, so to speak, and confess to my days as a cholesterol pusher on the streets of Calumet.

My job in that operation really began once the eggs were gathered in big wire baskets and brought into the basement egg room in the farmhouse. First the eggs had to be washed, then graded and packaged. We were fairly well mechanized for the times. Eggs were washed by placing the basket in an egg washing machine—a tub that sat on top of a machine that agitated the eggs in soapy water until clean. I would then "candle" each egg by holding it up to a light box to see if there were any flaws inside, then weigh it on a scale, and place it in the appropriately stamped carton—small, medium, large, extra-large or jumbos. As the size of the operation grew, so did the sophistication of our equipment with the purchase of a second-hand egg-grading machine. This processed the eggs much faster by placing the clean eggs on a little conveyor belt that moved them over a light for the inner check and then tipped them by weight so they sorted into the different sizes. Family legend has it that I got so good at this that I could grade eggs, read a book, eat a snack, and sometimes entertain my younger brother all at the same time.

While the packaging responsibilities were a daily chore, the marketing was done mostly on Friday evenings when my mother and I went on the "egg route" delivering door-to-door in the Calumet area. While in recent years my mother will admit that the whole "egg business" was not really to her liking, I found the rewards to outweigh the detriments most of the time. I liked the money because, in addition to what I earned for my packaging and delivery duties, I also made out quite well on tips from our grateful customers. In an ordinary week this could amount to a couple of dollars (and a lot more on a holiday week) which was not bad in an economic climate where the admission to the matinees at the Calumet Theatre was a quarter and Hershey bars still came in five- and ten-cent sizes.

The egg girl becomes Miss U.P. Farm Bureau (pictured with the late Gov. Romney)

I also liked the access that this gave me into the homes of the area. Calumet was then, and remains so to some extent today, a

Stirring It Up!

multi-ethnic community of small locations and neighborhoods and we delivered everywhere. Our route started in Raymbaultown (pronounced locally as Rambletown), the location on the south side of town named after a French priest who had been among the first settlers. We then would swing past the huge old Sacred Heart Church through Hecla location where there was a Croatian family that every Christmas would send out plates of pavatic (pronounced pa-va-teet-sa), that delicate bakery of many thin layers of pastry thick with nuts. We continued on into Florida location—and no, the temperature did not rise. Then we would visit a few of the farmhouses on the Lake Linden hill and it was on one of these stops that I received what is still one of the best compliments of my life.

On that day the family had a visitor from the city—a man of about seventy in age. Coffee was being served in the kitchen when I arrived with my eggs. As the housewife scurried off to get her purse to pay me the man looked me over and then said, "You look just like the girl of the Limberlost." I don't know how many other girls of my age even would have known who the Girl of the Limberlost was as the book was published in 1909. But somehow a very tattered copy of this had been my very favorite book. I loved Elnora, the very courageous (and beautiful) girl from the swamplands of Ohio who battled against multiple adversaries to earn her way through high school by selling her collections of butterflies and moths. She was a heroine for country girls everywhere.

Back up the hill we delivered on almost every street of Laurium. Here I remember several Finnish families who increased their order every year as the number of blond babies multiplied. After a brief detour into Albion Location on the far north side of town we got to Calumet proper with one of our first stops being a family we thought of as our "health nuts." They loved our fresh eggs because they consumed them raw. On through Blue Jacket, Yellow Jacket, Red Jacket (I have wondered for years how these "jacket" names came about and no one to date ever has had an answer) and then up the hill to Tamarack Location. Back down we dipped into the little Italian neighborhood around the then operative St. Mary's Church to deliver to an old Italian couple. I loved the smells in that kitchen—a rich mixture of garlic, basil and tomato sauce. Perhaps it was a premonition of the life I would lead with my Italian cook husband. From there it was up Swedetown Hill (mostly Finns there!) and finally home.

The only time when I didn't like to deliver was when it was to the homes of kids I knew from school, especially boys that I thought "cute." Somehow, visions of Elnora aside, the role of *egg girl* just didn't seem too glamorous. Otherwise, somewhat surprising since I was a shy kid, I enjoyed my customer relations. Of course I was supremely confident about the quality of the product. I knew those eggs were fresh, clean and had little chance of inner blemish, and people confirmed this with their repeat business and praise. One thing for sure—they were superior to any Wisconsin egg.

We held Wisconsin eggs in deep scorn and to this day I cannot comfortably eat eggs in what otherwise I always have found a pleasant enough state. This disdain was based on the fact that the eggs the markets brought from the wholesalers came out of Wisconsin and were never as fresh as our eggs. I remember shopping for groceries with my parents and how they always would check the egg section to see what price was being charged. This almost always was less than our price but then they were for Wisconsin eggs. Of course there always were some people who bought on price alone—so the hard economic realities were learned.

With all this time and energy spent on eggs as a business I don't remember that we ate them any more often than most families. Actually my mother, indulgent to her sons, would for several years fix my brother hamburgers for breakfast. (Okay, okay, she fixed me chicken noodle soup but it was canned.) She says now that her philosophy was to give us whatever we would eat in the morning so that there would be something in our stomachs before we trudged off into the cold Keweenaw winters—a woman ahead of the times.

But it was from my father that I learned to cook my favorite egg dish—simple scrambled eggs. He always stressed that eggs needed gentle handling. A dab of butter melted to coat the pan. The use of low heat. Whisking the eggs delicately. The addition of just a little milk to keep them soft. A pinch of salt and pepper. Focusing on the task so as not to overcook. The removing of the eggs to a plate just as they reached the point of being cooked through, fluffy, a pale yellow, no brown edges ever. The taking of time to sit at the kitchen table and enjoy the results. Perhaps he too was ahead of his time, for could even the most diligent cholesterol cause a problem after all of that?

—February 1998

There's something about spring

There's something about spring that makes me think that maybe I should not eat so much meat and concentrate on a vegetable diet. I've never been a particularly avid vegetable eater, but each year along about this time I think of gardens being cleaned of winter debris, spaded and turned in preparation for planting. Actually, when I think of these gardens two particularly come to mind. One is the big garden in the backyard at 821 North Third Street when it was my parents' place.

As soon as the snow was gone, my father began to clear the garden area of the accumulations of winter stuff. I helped whether I wanted to or not. I think it was more often "not" but even though my "nots" might work well with my indulgent grandmother or my mother, they never worked with my father. Garden plans each year changed as my father found new things that he wanted to grow. I remember particularly the year that he was promised some new tomato variety from a New York Central railroad friend he met in Mackinaw City, where the DSS&A met the N.Y. Central line. This new variety was the Rutgers University in New Jersy "beefsteak" tomato. I think we might have been one of the first families in Marquette to have this new tomato.

In those days the Marquette County Fair was held in the city at the fairgrounds which covered a large area at what was then the dead end of Lincoln Street where the National Guard Armory is (the harness racing track circled those Norway pines that still stand) and the grounds went as far to the west as the beginning of the Catholic Cemetary. I recall that each year for a number of years our Beefsteak tomatoes got first prize. Unlike today's unfortunate paucity of vegetable entries at the fair, because most people had home gardens to supplement their diets, the number of entries was amazing, as was the quality. I think first prize was seventy-five cents and in those dark days of the Depression this bought two pounds of butter and five loaves of Mother's Bread, six cents a loaf, sliced, from the A&P with some change left over for a Popsicle on a hot August day.

The second garden I think of at this time of year, in anticipation, is that of my friends Ted Bogdan and Maggie Linn. In some respects I like this one better as I don't do any work on it and Ted manages to grow some of the best stuff around and freely lets me taste it. Their vegetable garden, carefully planned, is enhanced (greatly) by Maggie's beautiful complementary flowering plants. But how could anyone who creates such beautiful watercolors produce anything but plants of beauty?

It has been lightly snowing as I write this and the snow cover is far from gone, but I feel confident that the snow will stop and the green will come again.

I think that one of the reasons I tire so quickly of vegetable dishes is the mostly unimaginative preparation methods. The vegetable preparations that follow are, it is hoped, somewhat different than the usual and I hope that they will lead you to test them. And, despite what I might have said in the past (something like "meat and potatoes are enough") these vegetables are very good and very good for your health I am told.

Stirring It Up!

• • •

Asparagus: In the not very distant past, an exotic vegetable, rarely available except in season. Now it is in the vegetable section of most stores seemingly all year long. It varies in price, by season, from not too bad to absolutely horrible. But as one doesn't need more than four or five on a plate to add color and class to something ordinary, and individually they are light in weight, cost of service is quite reasonable, even when they are expensive by the pound. Choose asparagus all of the same size and thickness. Cut off the very end, peel stalks only if they are large, cook in simmering water in a deep fry pan and remove before they become soggy. Drain. For *Asparagus Flamande* (one pound of asparagus) chop two hard cooked eggs finely, season with salt and pepper, melt one-quarter cup of butter. On service dish, sprinkle eggs, pour butter, serve.

• • •

Brussels Sprouts: A much maligned and overlooked vegetable, not to say one whose name is frequently mispelled is the Brussels sprout, a distinguished member of the cabbage family. First to be noted here is that the spelling of the vegetable is always with a capital "B," as in Brussels, the Belgian city giving name to them, which means there is always an "s" at the end. Frequently the name is incorrect on the store labels, not only in Marquette, but many other places. I suppose soon, in another generation, the capitalization will disappear and the ending "s" will be gone. (I am surprised that no one yet has named a teen-aged rap group after this vegetable. Let us hope that God will continue to intervene.) But for the time being, it is Brussels sprouts.

Buy fresh, green sprouts. Pull off any loose outer leaves. Trim stem end if needed and make fairly deep cross cuts in the stem, for more uniform cooking. You do not have to presoak them in lemon or vinegar water. Wash them briefly under running cold water. Simple preparation methods are best. Here are two wonderful ones:

Cook for eight to ten minutes in lots of boiling water until they are barely tender then drain quickly. For one and one-half pounds sprouts, melt about six tablespoons butter in a frying pan over medium heat, add the cooked and drained sprouts and roll them in the butter for a minute. Squeeze the juice of one lemon over them, put on serving platter, add a little salt and pepper. Enjoy.

You can turn these simple Brussels Sprouts in butter into *Brussels Sprouts Italiana* by following everything above and when you put them on the serving platter, sprinkle one-half cup of good, grated Parmesan cheese over them.

Simple is best.

• • •

Broccoli: (There IT is again.) Remember when President George Bush (the Elder) said that he didn't like broccoli? Some of us joined with him in his remarks. But remember, too, that he was only a one-term president. No one has asked the Kid yet if he likes broccoli.

Mostly broccoli is cooked in boiling water, salted or buttered or cheesed and served. Here is a little better way, I think. *Braised Broccoli Romana*. Get rid of any tough outer leaves—actually your store will have done that in most cases and if not, you pull them off before getting them weighed. Price is high enough without paying for debris. Cut off the stalks about two inches below the heads. Peel stalks, cut any thick stalks in half lengthwise or if they are very thick, quarter them. For two pounds of broccoli heat about four tablespoons of oil in a large skillet over medium heat, add two cloves of crushed garlic and cook until garlic begins to color. Add one cup of dry white wine and the broccoli stalks, season with a little salt and pepper, cover the pan and simmer for about five minutes. Now lay the heads of broccoli on top of the stalks, season again with a little salt and pepper and cook uncovered for about ten minutes longer or until both the stalks and heads are tender. If too much wine evaporates, add a little more but five minutes before the

Stirring It Up!

broccoli is cooked, raise the heat, reduce the liquid to about one-half cup. Arrange the broccoli on a serving platter and pour the liquid over.

Here, too, simple is best. Broccoli is most often spoiled by over cooking or over flavoring. Properly cooked, lightly flavored broccoli is very tasty and good.

I remember that former President Bush tried mightily to modify that anti-broccoli remark, but he didn't really succeed in molifying the Broccoli gods, I suspect.

• • •

Vegetables, properly handled, are very good. Now, in this Vegetable Apologia we are only at the very beginning of the alphabet of vegetables. I bet you can't wait until we get to Turnips and Zucchini, eh?

—March 2001

Bread: Its mystery & fascination

Recently I talked before a women's group about food. The planned topic was *Food, Art and Grace,* but as frequently happens with my food interest, the subject narrowed to bread. Several women at the supper table with me were home bread bakers and one of them had a "bread" machine. My dislike of this machine is precisely that it is a machine: ingredients in, close the door, set the time, take out the product. Not a bad idea for some foods, but bread has a spirit at work and the machine hides the spirit. If you don't believe that instinctively, I probably will be unable to persuade you.

Think about it for a moment. One takes some wheat which has been ground to a fine powder, adds some warm water, some yeast and some salt if one wishes, though it is not a necessary ingredient. (Some Tuscan breads served in Florence are salt-free.) Mix these together (if your yeast is newly purchased, you really don't even have to "proof" it) into a gooey mess. Dump it out of your mixing bowl and start to knead. If your recipe's proportions are right, you will begin to feel this strange mixture become "dough." It will no longer be flour, water, salt and yeast. It will begin to live, to display a force working against you—you press down and turn, the dough begins to acquire elasticity and to resist your pressing.

The Spirit has entered into the mixture, right before your eyes, brought there by your hands and by your skill in putting the right ingredients together. If you are a "bread person" you will feel the life under your hands. Set this new mixture aside and it will grow as you watch and if you are patient, it will grow to a new size and if you press it down and try to punch this new life out of the dough, it will grow again.

Now you put it into the oven and it continues to grow until the temperature is so high (about 135 degrees F.) that the yeast is killed and the loaf is stabilized. When baked, it becomes an important supporter of human life: in the morning, toast and rolls; at lunch, bread for sandwiches or with soups or salads; at evening, rolls with dinner. Bread is everywhere in our lives. I am a serious skeptic when it comes to miracles, but the production of a loaf of bread, worked by hand, seems to me to be so remarkable that it goes beyond mere obvious chemistry and sits at the very edge of awe.

The Egyptians "invented" yeast-leavened bread and that invention raised them above all other peoples in the ancient world. Most of the inhabitants of the ancient world lived on a cereal food made by roasting grains on hot stones with water to form a paste. Sometimes the paste was spread on hot stones until it was baked to a hard and tough sheet. This preserved it, but removed the taste. Porridge was made by heating the grain/water mixture over a fire. Porridge and flat breads, flat breads and porridge remained the food for many centuries. Even the Romans lived on porridge for a long time. If it wasn't for the people of Egypt, the world might never have known about bread.

The Egyptians did something significantly different in the handling of the grain and water mixture: most people cooked it to preserve it or threw it away. The Egyptians set some of the mixture aside to decay—or ferment as we now know. The process of fermentation was known for a long time and only understood in the

Stirring It Up!

seventeenth century when the Dutchman Van Leeuwenhock saw yeast as cells under his microscope. Pasteur proved that yeast is a living organism. The early Egyptians didn't know this, but they did know that when they baked the funny smelling fermented mixture, the product was like nothing else ever tasted. They also knew that this new product could not be baked on the coals of an open fire, so by trial and error, they constructed the first bread oven.

From time to time, one will hear of some baker (it happened to me just recently) say that all his bread contains is flour, water and salt, there is no yeast. What he (or she) means is that no commercial yeast, in a package, was added to the bread. But, of course, if one makes a leavened loaf of yeast bread there is yeast in it. The air around us contains bacteria and yeast spores, just looking for a place to land for nourishment. If you mix some water and flour and let it remain out, uncovered, for eight to twenty-four hours, you will find that it begins to bubble, pick up some movement, and smell sour. Fermentation has begun and you are on the way to producing sour dough starter. This starter, added to your flour, water and salt mixture becomes the "yeast." And if you don't wish to go through this process each time you make a new loaf of bread, you can save some of the "starter" and begin a new starter. Thus sour dough starters in the olden days were of great value and were transported all across our country—which is how we got San Francisco sour dough bread. The gold miners of the 1840s helped this bread become famous, of course.

After the Fleischmann brothers brought fresh yeast to America from Europe in the 1860s and with the invention of active dried yeast in World War II, there was very little need for the sour dough starter, except for its unusual taste and a kind of food religion that has grown up around it. The use of baking powders became popular in the 1850s in this country as an antidote for yeast, thought by some "health" fanatics to be poisonous, Sylvester Graham among them. But the various baking powders soon were limited to the thin mixes such as griddle cakes, and for quickbreads, muffins and biscuits. This is where things stand now. As the last word on leavening, it should be pointed out here that some commercial breads are mechanically aerated and yeast is only added for flavor. Whipping a dough is quicker than waiting for yeast for grow.

Well, I've strayed again. I started out with the intention of noting that Marquette is in the beginning of a baking renaissance. Trenary Home Bakery and DJ's probably are our oldest old-fashioned bakeries. The current interest in more European and so-called health food bakeries was begun by the Sweet Water Cafe a few years ago. The newest addition is the very large variety of breads produced by a bakery on South Front Street, formerly the Mister Donut shop and now the Donut Hole and the Huron Mountain Bread Co.

—June 1997

Bread: Forgotten art form?

My thesis for this short column (my publisher robbed me of space to accept additional advertising!) is that the making of bread is an art. J. E. Jacob in his 1944 treasure *6000 Years of Bread* says that the "mystical marriage and transformation of matter...the mystery of the creation of bread" has all but vanished from our culture. Those of you who have combined flour, water, yeast and salt into a gooey mess and through some strange alchemy produced a tantalizing, crusty, chewy incredibly elegant smelling loaf of bread know what he's writing about.

So, think of this piece as a plea to keep alive the mystery of bread in an age of accelerating cultural diminishment. More and more, material and services are just a little bit less costly and of a lot less quality.

Bread quite possibly is the oldest manufactured food known to humans. It always has been closely associated with religion as well as tradition. In Rome's time, a bread stamp (tressara frumentaria) was issued to the poor of Rome so that they could get adequate bread. It was molded of bronze and had the ruling emperor's outline on it. Was this the first food stamp? Human protein sources mostly were grain; in times of great famine in the Middle Ages, people did some desperate things to try to get nutrition: in France, earth was mixed with a little flour and eaten. The worst famine breads were Swedish (they still are preserved in museums) and consisted of ninety percent pine bark and straw.

Bread baking requires mixing, kneading and fermentation. At home these steps require several hours. In large commercial bakeries, where time and work are money, mechanical dough developers can produce a "ripe" dough in four minutes. Yeast is added only as a flavoring.

This is part of the process of diminishment that I noted above. Around our area there are several small bakeries (DJ's, Babycakes, Trenary Home Bakery, etc.) which produce some good breads. Supermarkets and other stores use frozen dough (mostly) and from this some very good bread is produced.

Pain ordinaire, the French bread of romance, consists only of flour, water, yeast and salt. It has no added fat. If you add some olive oil to it, you get a loaf of fine Italian bread. In any case, the following recipe calls for olive oil. I use white flour here because that's what it is "supposed" to be. You can use up to twenty percent whole-wheat flour if you wish. (No, you do not necessarily get more nutrition from whole-wheat flour—in fact you may get less. Whole wheat may begin with more inherent nutrients, but it does not remain in your body's extraction system as long, thus you expel nutrients. There is an old saying, a version of which began with Hippocrates in 400 B.C., which paraphrased, says: white for nutrition, dark for laxative.)

First, get a baguette pan, easily obtainable in local kitchen supply stores. Some are dark metal and some a shiny metal. It doesn't really matter in this case, though the dark cooks a little quicker.

• • •

Stirring It Up!

For two large loaves or four smaller baguettes:

2 C. hot water—110 degrees F.
2 packages active dry yeast or 1-1/2 Tbls. of same
2 tsp. salt
1 Tbls. olive oil
5-1/2 C. all purpose flour (American "bread flour" is a hard, or higher protein, flour, but French bread flour is a softer flour, so use all purpose)

If you have one, use a mixer with a dough hook, if not, do it by hand. I'm not going to describe the process so that I don't go over my too small space.

Place the water in a large bowl; add yeast, mix to dissolve, but do not beat or stir too much. Let yeast "proof" since this is part of the fun and magic. You do not need sugar for yeast to grow; when yeast is growing (you'll know it), add the salt and oil. Now add the flour, all at once or in several batches. Mix and knead well, until dough is integrated, shiny and somewhat resistant to your kneading.

Place in another very lightly oiled bowl, cover and let it rise in a warm place—up to 80 degrees F. The colder the rise, the better the flavor.

When dough has doubled in size, punch it down, cut it in two or four parts, form into long loaves and place in lightly oiled pans; you can use a spray can if you wish. That way you will tend to use less fat and also not affect the flavor as much.

Let it rise again (about twenty-five to thirty minutes), slash loaves in three places with razor blade, sprinkle very lightly with flour and place it in the oven.

Your oven should have been preheated earlier to 450 degrees F. and there should be a pan of water in the bottom, steaming when you place the bread pans in. (This bread will not bake properly at any temperature less that 450 degrees F.) After ten minutes, take the pan of water out. (The steam keeps a crust from forming quickly on the bread, thus permitting a higher rise before internal temperatures of 140 degrees F. kill the yeast.) These loaves will be baked in about twenty-five to forty minutes. Take them out, check that the bottoms are brown enough, place on wire rack to cool. Eat.

• • •

Do not place bread in plastic wrappers as this softens the crust, one of the best parts of the loaf. If you have one left the next day, place it back in the oven (at 350 degrees F.) for about five to six minutes. This will refresh it, but you can only do this once.

Do not refrigerate—one day at 46 degrees F. is equivalent in staling to five to six days at 75 degrees F. You can, however, quick freeze in plastic bags, thaw in the bag and then reheat as noted, outside of the bag, of course.

If you do this baking regularly and come to enjoy the ceremony of it, you will become very adept and all of this will go quickly. It is a great enjoyment to eat really good, home baked bread.

—August 1992

Soup and bread

I spend a lot of my "food time" thinking about, writing about, and experimenting with bread and soup. This column is about soup, though in food history, soup and bread are intimately linked. It would be difficult, I think, to find two basic foods with more variations than these products. Go to your favorite supermarket and check out the soup and bread varieties. As you might already know, most of these supermarket products, whether canned or dried, taste pretty good. Commercial suppliers to restaurants and institutions stock soups and soup bases and related products by the hundreds—I am looking at one supplier's computer printout of soup and bases totalling more than five full pages, over a hundred varieties and makers. Read the ingredient list on soup cans to find the following examples: (in a beef barley soup) bleached flour, hydrolyzed corn and wheat, soy protein, maltodextrin, corn oil, caramel color, whey and "natural flavor"—whatever that is. So, the soup has a lot of "additives," but are they unhealthy, do they enhance the flavor and does the soup taste good?

Most breads today are made also with help from manufacturer's bases and are not "real" bread in the old fashioned sense—or are these two most popular foods now merely manufactured products? Surely. This is the way we have been going forever. Things change; foods, even those we like to think of as unchanging, are modified to meet the needs of changing culture. It is not difficult to make soup at home, nor is it difficult to make bread at home. How many people do you know who do it? It is interesting particularly to note that both bread and soup modifications are designed to make the user think he is getting a "real" product, not one that is modified. The line between "real" and "manufactured" certainly has been blurred. In preparation for this column I looked for something "natural," no fat, "healthy" to test the so-called "health food" supply. I did find a can of "chicken broth" labeled as all natural, fat-free, low-sodium for $1.35 for 14.5 ounces. This product is so bad that I think it is important to note the brand to warn you: *Shelton's Chicken Broth* lists its ingredients as "chicken broth, dehydrated onion, dehydrated celery and natural spices." Quite healthy sounding. The problem is that any chicken taking part in manufacture of this product only walked past the pot, perhaps dipping a foot in on the way by. This product tastes like warm water. I suppose it's healthy. On the other hand, I found Shari's Bistro Organic Tomato with Roasted Garlic Soup (fat free) $2.05 for fourteen and one-half ounces to be quite tasty. One can did contain nineteen percent of your daily salt need, however.

I have tied bread and soup together here because they go together historically.

The word soup is said to derive from the Germanic *sop,* which originally meant the bread over which the broth or other liquid was poured. It is probable that *sup* and *supper* are related words. I read recently that today in some regions of France *la soupe* refers to the crust of bread with which the liquid—*le potage*—is served. Bread is such an integral part of soup that there still exist recipes, which require only that hot water be poured over bread with some herbs added.

Examples of this simple recipe are legion, but there are several variations I have tried which work very well. First there is a French (and Italian) version which is made by using stale bread, torn into large pieces, with boiling water poured over, then whisked into a near-puree. Then it is finished off by adding butter and egg yolks, for enrichment. There seems little doubt that the original soup was just the bread and water. The first and most simple variation on the soup is the use of a broth instead of just water; next one adds some flavor, such as sauteing sliced leeks in butter.

The Italians have a wonderful variation of this basic bread soup romantically named Zuppa di Cipolle e Pane, or more prosaically, *Onion and Bread Soup*. This is very simple to make and is in fact a famous soup served at Il Latini, a trattoria of great deserved fame in Florence. Start with a big pile of thinly sliced red onions (about eight large), using a large ovenproof casserole or sauce pan, cook the onions slowly, stirring frequently until they are soft and reduced in volume. Sprinkle with one tablespoon of sugar and mix well. Add six cups of a rich chicken broth and the same amount of a very dry white wine. Add a cinnamon stick, bring to a boil. Place in a 350 degree F. oven, covered, for one hour. Remove the cover, add six thick slices of Italian bread (day old is best) torn into pieces. Cook uncovered for thirty minutes in the oven. Remove from oven, take out the cinnamon stick, and whisk the bread until it is amalgamated with the broth and wine. Serve with Parmesan cheese.

While I am on the bread/soup tack, I should not neglect the great *bread and broth soup* made with the addition of saffron to the chicken broth and layering bread slices with slices of chicken breast, some carrot rounds, all baked in the oven until the whole thing is cooked. After it is baked, if it still seems a little dry, just add some more broth or hot water.

None of the above suggestions for soup need detailed recipes; get the ingredients, use your own judgment and make some soup.

There seems little doubt that soup, however the first very simple product started, grew in variety and complexity as resources became more available and human ingenuity figured out the use of one new product after another. But, while human ingenuity is wonderful for the acquisition of new ingredients and their mix, we humans seem always to want to do things quicker, cheaper and with less work. And therein lie the problem.

Quicker and cheaper for the end user can mean a loss of quality. But, it is not too difficult to make some broth at home, store it in your freezer for use when you need it. Chicken broth is easier to make than good beef stock, so try this method:

Chicken Broth
(To make 4 quarts)
Two 3-1/2 lb. chickens, cut in half so they will fit in a stock pot
1 large onion cut into quarters
1 large garlic bulb, unpeeled
A bouquet garni made of tarragon, bay leaf and parsley
5 quarts of water
Some coarse salt

Put the chicken in a stock pot, place the vegetables and the bouquet garni around the chicken. Pour in the water to cover and slowly bring to a boil. Using a slotted spoon or other skimmer, skim the surface until no more scum forms on the top. As the fat rises, skim that, too. When the boiling point is reached, add a little salt and cover the pot, setting lid ajar, reduce the heat and cook undisturbed for about two hours. Remove the solids and drain the broth through several thicknesses of cheesecloth in a colander.

With a store of good chicken broth in your freezer, you won't need to buy canned soups. There are many good cookbooks with soup recipes, healthful and easy to make. But it also is fun to start with a simple broth and invent your own soup, being aware when you start that probably someone before you has come up with a similar soup.

Here are two recipes prepared by a local cook mostly because he was bored with standard recipes and there was stuff needing to be used before it became waste:

Stirring It Up!

Ten-Curve Bean Soup
1 pound 10-bean mix
1/2 tsp. cayenne pepper
3 Tbls. medium hot sauce
1 pkg. frozen spinach, thawed and chopped
1 8-oz. jar roasted red peppers, chopped small
1 tsp. black pepper
16 cups chicken stock
1 tsp. dried oregano

Prepare beans, rinse away cooking liquid. Add chicken stock, peppers and spinach to the rinsed beans and bring to a boil. Now add the remaining ingredients and simmer for one hour.

Confetti Vegetable
6 medium zucchini, cut into medium pieces
6 summer squash, cut into medium pieces
1 8-oz. jar roasted red peppers, chopped into 1/4-inch dice
8 C. water
8 carrots, chopped medium
3 Tbls. dried dill weed
2 Tbls. chopped garlic
2 Tbls. sea salt
1/4 lb. butter

Melt butter in a stockpot, add the cut-up vegetables and saute for three to five minutes. Add the water and bring to a boil and cook until the carrots are tender. Add dill, garlic, salt and process in a food processor until vegetables are chopped small but not paste.
Have fun.

—August 1997

Stirring It Up!

Summerthyme
Patricia J. Tikkanen

This is the third year for my small herb garden and I am learning some lessons in unmanageability. Catnip has sprouted into a bush crowding Greek Oregano and Sage into a corner. Sweet Cicely is shading Lavendar. Gray Artemisia has integrated (invaded?) Thyme, Mint has overshadowed completely poor Rosemary and Comfrey (and oh, I was warned about Comfrey!) soon will dominate my whole third tier. Things are clearly (and gloriously) out of control.

I have to admit that I love it this way. While I'm sure that some may see this as the sign of a disorganized character, I have forgiven myself entirely. After all, the first year of any garden is always more drudge than delight and my patch's second year was last summer when nothing in the Upper Peninsula grew out of control (except perhaps political egos). Not that this garden was ever as barren as my first attempt a few years ago.

At that time I was living on a corner lot and after being given a beautiful gardening book (*The Complete Book of Gardening* edited by Michael Wright and published by Warner Books) for Christmas

I decided to plant flower borders around my two "public" sides. I planned these gardens all winter, reading and rereading the section on garden planning and carefully diagramming the beds.

I was thrilled once the seeds arrived in the local stores and remember spending several hours (one while a March sleet storm raged outside) picking out package after package of seeds. At home I arranged these on the living room floor according to my diagrams imagining how they would look once they were all in bloom. Better I had read the chapter on "gardening techniques and technicalities" that featured subtitles like "understanding your soil," "plant disorders" and "supporting your plants." I didn't. It sounded too much like one of my social work textbooks and besides, I reasoned, I'm predisposed genetically to flower gardening. I'm sure that one of the first things my Finnish grandmother did on our Copper Country farm was plant her rose bushes and day lilies. So, one Saturday in May I planted all those seeds.

I don't think I had a single bloom on anything that year. This was embarrassing particularly since I had talked about these flower beds for months and friends kept driving by waiting to see the results. I did learn: No. 1, one of the great joys of gardening is the winter "plotting" with seed catalogues and garden books; No. 2, greenhouses that sell nice, healthy starter plants are there for a reason.

These lessons have served me well in starting my second garden after a move. Again, some of the impetus came from a Christmas gift, *The Complete Book of Herbs* by Lesley Bremness (Viking Studio Books). The idea of an herb garden interested me because it seemed like a nice complement to the skills of my husband, Don (Curto), in the kitchen. I liked the idea that what I grew would be useful.

Herbs somehow seem like a nice balance between the total decadence of flowers and the self-righteous virtues of vegetables. Having said that, I need to admit to still being as interested in flash

Stirring It Up!

as in flavor. My absolutely favorite herb right now is my silver tansy with tiny, daisy-like flowers. The chef, of course, has a different point of view. In fact, there have been a few threats from him against that catnip I mentioned (masses of delicate lavendar flowers but of major interest for consumption only to felines) interfering with two culinary mainstays like sage and oregano.

Actually he doesn't complain much because he's busy figuring ways to use what is produced. For the cook this is the time of year for abandon when herbs can be measured by the handful rather than teaspoon. One of Don's quick favorites is taking a whole frying-size *chicken,* separating the skin from the meat along the breast sides and inserting whole, plush stems of fresh *tarragon.* The tarragon is removed after baking but what remains is the flavor.

Another entree idea, and an innovation this summer, was l*emon balm steamed fish.* Lemon balm was new to us with this garden and has turned out to be a delightful cousin to the better known mints. Don likes a tea made from its leaves although he only has nasty things to say about the usual mint teas I drink all year. This may be because my herb book mentions that in the thirteenth century drinking lemon balm tea was associated with long life. According to the book, a man named John Hussey of England was reported to have lived to be 116 years old after fifty years of drinking lemon balm tea with honey for breakfast.

While this drink *has not* replaced our morning coffee, the fish is excellent. Again, to really infuse the flavor you need several good size pieces of plant for each piece of fish. Actually this technique can be used with any fish or with chicken breasts and any herb you think will be tasty. Merely place the meat or fish on a tray in the steamer and lay some fresh herbs over it. The amount depends upon how powerful you wish the flavor of the herb to be. Test it for yourself. But it is pretty difficult to spoil this recipe, so go ahead and be bold rather than timid. You may note that both the fish and the chicken recipes call for no added fat and need no sauce—a real plus if your household, like ours, is now on the "fat makes fat" plan.

Herbal abandon also means a certain daring in mixing handfuls of different herbs in the same dish. We have found *salads* to be an excellent place for experimenting. For a Fourth of July potluck I mixed a good two cups of chopped and torn herbs including mint, lemon balm, tarragon, oregano, basil and sage (leaves *and* flowers) with about one-and-a-half heads of bibb lettuce, sweet red and yellow peppers and half of a sweet onion. Arugula (a real peppery salad herb I've since added) would have been good too. I tossed this with a classic vinaigrette to which I didn't add any herbs which was the only suggestion from the Chef. Apparently one gets a better suspension if there are some solids for the oil and vinegar to associate with—sort of like hanging together. The salad was a hit, competing well with the more traditional picnic foods.

Another dish that lends itself to this kind of recklessness is pasta. Here are Don's directions for a kind of *mystery pasta* with infinite variations. Proportions, he says, are "your own good cooking sense."

"In a large frying pan over medium heat place a half tablespoon each of butter and olive oil; when melted add some (lots of) finely chopped garlic, a small amount of red pepper flakes, a couple of slices of fresh tomato chopped medium, a tablespoon or two of good thick cream and some salt and pepper. Mix well and cook briefly. Take a pile of already cooked angel hair pasta and dump it in the pan. Mix well, place in serving bowl and cover with a whole handful of chopped and mixed oregano, basil, Italian parsley, tarragon and even sage if you are really daring. Mix gently and serve. The smell will set your head spinning."

And, speaking of head-spinning smells, it is time for the harvesting of basil and this seems to be a good year for it. In our house the summer of 1992 came to be known as *The Summer Without Basil.* For an Italian this seems to be a tragedy on a par with the Irish potato famine, so as you might imagine, this summer we are eating everything (except our "fat-free-sugar-free-ice-cream-like-substance") with basil. This pungent herb is great in scrambled eggs, chopped on tomatoes with oil and vinegar, or mixed into most salads.

However, some cooks would argue that basil really was put on this earth for the making of pesto sauce. According to Don, pesto is sort of like chicken soup, each family has its own variation and swears that it alone is God's very own pronouncement. Still, he was willing to pass on his directions.

"*Pesto* is traditionally made in a mortar with a pestle—but then writing formerly was done on waxed tablets before the computer was invented—so get out your food processor; place two tablespoons pine nuts in it and grind them down; dump in at least two cups of tightly packed fresh (washed very thoroughly) basil leaves—no stems. Add some salt and pepper, about three cut up cloves of fresh garlic and three-quarters cup of good olive oil (this is not the place to skimp on quality of oil—get good extra virgin oil). Process to a well-balanced liquid and, if you plan to freeze, stop here. The cheeses go in just before using. Cheese measure for each amount recited above is one-half cup Parmesan, plus two tablespoons Asiago. Coat hot cooked pasta with some of this sauce, which can be thinned a bit with some hot pasta water. A dollop of pesto dropped into hot thick vegetable soup is pretty good stuff, too."

Now, if I could just get him to think of some way to use all that catnip.

—August 1993

Potluck
Patricia J. Tikkanen

About this time last year I was considering a social movement dedicated to the elimination of the potluck. I was going to call it SOP (Stamp Out Potlucks). A harsh sentence, perhaps, for this time-honored tradition but I was beginning to feel desperate. I even had found a few compatriots—a few of you who never may have loved potluck fare, but found yourself remembering fondly those tuna casseroles, seven-layer salads, and date bars as you made your way through a buffet of cartons of fried chicken lumps, plastic containers of grocery store potato salad and a bag of potato chips. As I had it figured, the problem was fairly simple. No one had the time to cook any more, so why didn't we just admit it and, if we feel compelled to eat together, do the civilized thing by ordering pizza.

Well, fortunately or not, a few of the groups I'm affiliated with had some good potluck meals with honest homemade stuff and, as my disillusionment faded, I lost my zeal. (Lest I lose my status with the Marquette Writers Group I must add here that their potlucks are among the best I have ever attended, proving that writers either are good cooks or, more to the point for some of us, marry good cooks.) Still, while I am no longer planning to organize a campaign for the demise of the potluck, I think it is time for us to reassess this culinary custom and return to the traditional potluck values that have made this a great custom.

First, and perhaps most importantly, potluck offerings must be (or at least appear to be) homemade. Now I understand that there may be days when there just isn't time to prepare something. (For us non-cooks read this as "days when you cannot convince the family cook to whip-up something for you." Personally, this is not a problem I have. Since my husband is well-known among our friends and acquaintances as the cook in the family even a hint that I might "pick something up" for a potluck, or even worse make something myself, immediately has him cooking or baking my contribution since he feels, justifiably, that he will get credited with anything I contribute anyway.) When you really can't produce something, then it's time to practice a little creative deception, such as putting that deli salad in your grandmother's old mixing bowl, garnishing it with some fresh parsley, and when asked for the recipe saying, "I'd love to give it to you but I really don't use a recipe. I just throw things together until they look right." I would suggest, however, that this will not work with any product advertised on national television.

The second value I suggest may create some real anxiety in the more timid. I propose that potlucks should in fact be "potluck," and that attempts to control it beyond the old "bring a dish to pass" are tampering with the very essence of the tradition. According to historical references, the word "potluck" first appeared in print in 1592, used by Thomas Nashe, a student at Cambridge University. It referred to the custom of the day of keeping a large iron pot of stew simmering over the open fire, which changed character from day to day depending on what ingredients were available. If an unexpected guest appeared, he was invited to "take potluck"—in other words, to share in the every day meal of the household. (The French phrase *pot au feu*, or "pot over the fire," shares the same origins and now is used to refer to an ordinary family meal. The Irish had a similar concept in their "pot of hospitality."

And so, historically, there is to be some *risk* associated with a potluck. Potluck hosts and hostesses who try to orchestrate the meal with lists and the assignment of dishes need to understand that what they end up with may be a very good meal but it is not potluck. (I would make an exception for some of the "theme" potlucks I've heard about over the years, which seems to me to have more than enough risk involved. Actually, the one where garlic had to season every dish sounds aromatic and probably quite successful from a culinary point of view. And certainly zucchini is versatile enough to appear in every course. But the one where only dishes including *beets* were allowed? Well, at any rate it certainly would be vibrant.)

Actually I used to believe in trying to organize potlucks myself, convinced that if there wasn't a plan of who was supposed to bring what we would end up with eight pasta salads or maybe nothing but chocolate stuff (perhaps not really a very big problem for some of us). What I've learned however is that even if you do get a perfectly balanced list there always are a few who will mess it up. There will be one who will not remember that he was down for meatballs and so brings a lemon cake. Another will have gone on a diet after promising a batch of triple chocolate fudge bars and so brings carrot sticks and another who was out of one of the essential ingredients for the promised casserole and substitutes a fruit salad. You might as well just let go and trust in the Saint of Potlucks. You don't think there is a Saint of Potlucks? Well, perhaps not. But then how can you possibly explain the fact that no matter what the number of participants you almost always will end up with about one-third bringing salads, another third contributing main dishes, one or two people bringing bread, and the rest contributing desserts?

The last value I suggest that is essential to the preservation of the potluck is that of the enthusiastic eater. This role is so important that I suggest that if your group contains too many "restrained eaters" you may want to invite a few people who have this gift, letting them know that their contribution is to eat what the rest of you provide. While most enthusiastic eaters seem to have been born that way, there is some evidence that it is a skill that can be taught. One of the best enthusiastic eaters I know is a friend who spent many years of his life in the clergy. He claims that the ability to negotiate a potluck line was an essential skill in the profession as "highly charged political events" at which he had learned that he had best not only sample every dish but find some compliment about each one.

Even with specially invited enthusiastic eaters, however, it still is necessary for each diner to do his or her part in this if potlucks are to survive. Too many people mentally counting fat grams and picturing that food pyramid as they fill their plates will mean its demise.

In summary, it is best to make at least three comments about the quality and appearance of the food while serving yourself, leave the table with a plate that looks like as much food as you ordinarily would eat at two meals, exclaim over the taste of at least two items, and ask for at least one recipe. Anything less than this just will not do.

• • •

If you want to be remembered
There are three basic strategies for being remembered after your next potluck invitation—soup, homemade bread, or chocolate.

Soup actually is an unusual contribution to a potluck and so you get noticed for originality right off. This is a particularly welcome addition during the cold months here in the Upper Peninsula when our high proportion of soup lovers is at their most vocal. One bit of bother however, is that you really need to bring disposable bowls and spoons as the host usually will not be equipped with these. My Chef Consultant suggests the following Zucchini Soup, which is easy to make, can be doubled or even tripled with no problems, and which he promises will be remembered long after the contributions of others are forgotten.

Zucchini Soup
3 C. rich chicken broth
1-1/2 lbs. zucchini, scrubbed, trimmed and chopped
1 large onion, sliced thin
3 Tbls. olive oil
1-1/2 Tbls. curry powder (reduce when doubling)
Plain croutons and sour cream as as accompaniment

Make the soup: In large saucepan, bring the broth to boil with two and one quarter cups water, add the zucchini and simmer until zucchini is tender.
In skillet, cook the onion in the oil over moderately low heat until the onion is soft and *not* browned. Add the curry powder and cook the mixture, stirring, for one minute.
In blender or food processor, puree the onion mixture with the zucchini mixture in batches and season the soup with salt and pepper.
Serve the soup hot, chilled or at room temperature with croutons and dollops of sour cream.

• • •

Homemade bread is another natural to get yourself noticed in the potluck crowd.

Italian-Style Bread
This is a fairly easy recipe which makes an unusually tasty and tender bread. It is possible to vary this recipe by using part whole-wheat and part all purpose white. One-half cup rye can be substituted for one cup of flour. (I find it particularly good with one-fifth whole-wheat, four-fifths white.) All other procedures remain the same.

For two long loaves:
1-1/2 Tbls. active dry yeast
1 Tbls. sugar
2 C. water—100-115 degrees F.
1 Tbls. salt
5-6 C. flour (Make 1 cup whole-wheat for good variation or use about 1/2 cup light rye instead of the whole-wheat)
4 Tbls. olive oil
Cornmeal to use on pan to keep bread from sticking.
Egg/water wash

Procedures: Combine yeast, sugar, water and allow to proof. After proofing begins (at froth stage) add olive oil.

Mix salt thoroughly with flour and add to yeast mixture in five batches, approximately. Stir until dough is stiff. Knead until no longer sticky—about ten minutes. (The "no longer sticky" is more important than the time estimate.)

Let rise until doubled. Punch down, knead again briefly, let rise one more time.

Take dough from bowl, punch down, divide into two parts. Form in loaves, place on baking sheet covered with cornmeal.

Let rise until loaves about double. Slash loaves in three places with razor or sharp knife, brush with lightly beaten egg white/water mixture.

Place in *cold oven* set for 375 degrees F. and bake for about thirty-five to forty minutes until done.

Let cool on racks. Enjoy.

• • •

The last strategy is chocolate. Almost anything chocolate will be appreciated and in fact there are some who would claim that a potluck without at least one chocolate dessert is by definition a failure no matter how good the rest of the dishes. Our suggestion...

Chocolate Cream Cake
4 eggs
1 C. sugar
1 C. all purpose flour
7/8 C. heavy whipping cream
4 oz. bitter-sweet chocolate, *grated*

Preheat oven to 375 degrees F. Butter an eight-inch round cake pan that is at least two inches deep, or use an eight-inch springform pan.

In a mixing bowl, beat the eggs and sugar until the mixture is very smooth. Mix in the flour. Stir in the cream and chocolate.

Transfer the batter to the prepared pan and bake for forty-five minutes. Let the cake cool in the pan for ten minutes, then turn the cake out onto a rack to cool completely. Serves six.

—February 1997

To shake or not to shake

For about fifty years it has been understood by anyone who could read that too much salt in one's diet was potentially dangerous to one's health. Often it was very difficult to guess just what "too much" meant without a milligram measurer in your pocket. Restricting salt has become part of the dogma and folklore of eating. Table salt once was held in such low regard (and fear) that these important institutions took part in warnings about the dangers of eating salt: the Food and Drug Administration, the American Heart Association, the American Medical Association and the Surgeon General's Office.

Salt's position in our diet is being reevaluated and the pendulum is swinging more in the favor of salt. There seems to be evidence that too little salt might be dangerous to the health of some people. It's apparent from the four or five condensations of studies that I've read that for those persons who have high blood pressure (hypertension) a restriction on the use of salt is in order if their physician prescribes such a regimen. As put in a report in the *Journal of the American Medical Association* (*JAMA*) in May of 1996: "Dietary restriction for older hypertensive individuals might be considered, but the evidence in the normotensive population does not support current recommendations for universal dietary restriction."

I don't have any desire to enter into the salt controversy—is it good or is it bad?—except to note that when renowned experts disagree over such seemingly simple matters, it is a good idea to take a middle road. I use about as much salt in my diet now as I did twenty years ago. It generally seems agreed that body weight reduction and not smoking are far more significant than salt restriction in preventing stroke and heart attacks. There even are studies which show that "cholesterol levels rise in seventy to eighty percent of people on a low-salt diet, increasing their risk of cardiovascular disease," according to Dr. Alexander Logan, professor of medicine, University of Toronto.

Salt is everywhere in foods: salt is a flavor enhancer, helping to bring out the natural flavors and it is a good preservative, retarding the growth of bacteria. Salt also gives proper texture to processed meats, cheeses, and bread. Salt acts as a control agent to regulate the rate of fermentation in processing pickles, sauerkraut, sausage, cheese and bread dough. As a rule, the more heavily processed a product is the more salt present.

Salt sounds like a chemical unit, but it actually is two chemicals: sodium (forty percent) and chloride (sixty percent) and without going into the chemistry of things it is worth noting that our bodies cannot survive without both these chemicals. So, it isn't a matter of salt or not salt, but a matter of how much.

Salt has an interesting history. It was exchanged for slaves in ancient Greece and this gave rise to the expression "not worth his salt." Special salt rations given to Roman soldiers were known as *salarium argentum*, which eventually became our word "salary."

Salt also had military significance. When Napolean's troops were retreating from Moscow, thousands died because their wounds would not heal as their diet lacked salt. The Erie Canal which opened

Stirring It Up!

in 1825 was sometimes known as "the ditch that salt built" because salt, a bulky product presenting major transportation difficulties, was originally the principal cargo transported via the canal.

The essential nature of salt has, through the years, subjected it to government control and monopoly. In Britian, special salt taxes supported the monarchy and thousands of Britishers were imprisoned for smuggling salt. The scarcity of salt was a major contributing cause to the French Revolution. There are more than thirty references to salt in the Bible, including the "salt of the Earth" reference.

Today, salt is so readily available and so cheap that it's hard to recall its importance in other lands and other times. We are fortunate that salt deposits are so common and so large. The largest known deposits in the United States are located in Louisiana, Texas, New York, Ohio, Michigan and Kansas. Michigan's largest deposits are in Manistee and St. Clair counties. It might come as a surprise to you (as it did to me) that only about four percent of the salt produced in North America reaches our dining tables. The largest percent of salt produced, about seventy percent, is used in the chemical industry. The rest is used for clearing streets and highways of ice and snow and some is used to stabilize soil.

Salt is produced mainly by three methods:

1) mining, similar to coal mining where shafts are sunk into the salt deposit, usually about 600 to 2000 feet below the surface. Salt is blasted loose, crushed and delivered to the surface;

2) brine evaporation, which involves drilling a hole into a salt deposit, flushing with water and driving the brine (slurry) to the surface through a companion pipe. The slurry is then dried, producing salt;

3) Solar Salt. Simply put, this process uses sunlight to evaporate water from pools of salt water, leaving the salt to be harvested. This method is used in only three locations in the United States, San Diego, San Francisco and the Great Salt Lake in Utah.

Most salt sold in the U.S., especially in the midwest, is "iodized salt" or plain salt which contains a tiny amount of iodine, a substance which the body requires to prevent goiter and its attendant ugly swelling of the throat. Iodine was first introduced into salt in 1924. This method of iodine treatment was selected because salt was used universally and everyone would thus get some of the necessary iodine. As a result, goiter virtually is eliminated in North America.

More than two million tons of salt each year goes to agricultural use, mostly into feed for animals or into salt blocks. Blocks are used in wild game management, too. In fact, the Salt Institute reports that there are more than 14,000 uses of salt and apparently our grandparents knew most of them. Here's a sampling:

• Salt added to water makes it boil at a higher temperature.
• Boiling eggs in salted water will make them peel easier.
• Salt tossed on a grease fire will smother flames.
• After washing cutting boards with soap and water, rub them with a damp cloth dipped in salt and the boards will be brighter and lighter.

I don't plan to list all 14,000 uses, but there is one that holds hope for those of you who got a tattoo and now regret it. The Salt Institute notes with caution that this is a medical procedure and needs to be done by a physician. It is called salabrasion and requires several treatments by rubbing salt on the tattoo. Healing is required between treatments but there is virtually no scarring. Talk to your doctor.

Salt also plays a part in many superstitions, centuries old. As everyone knows there are many situations where one should throw salt over one shoulder or the other for good luck or to prevent catastrophe. There is an old saying that it is very unlucky to not have salt in the house. There are many sayings about borrowing salt and being advised to not repay it—bad luck if you do apparently. There also is an ancient prohibition against burning salt. My favorite saying is the one which proclaims that if you burn salt you will be forced to pick up every grain of it out of Hell when you die.

—June 1998

Snowed in
Patricia J. Tikkanen

Growing up on the Keweenaw I was taught not to give in easily to the snow.

The schools didn't close very often in the 1950s and I remember trudging through some pretty thick white stuff "up to the mailbox" where the bus would pick up me and my brother. Some mornings we would be left waiting, shivering in spite of being wrapped in many layers, our eyes focused on the crest of the Golf Course hill, a half-mile across the white terrain, waiting for the hint of yellow haze that would mean the bus was climbing to the top of the other side and soon would come into our view. We could then watch it descend toward us, cautiously maneuvering the treacherous Olsons' Corner where someone from our family was bound to get stuck at least once every winter. Somehow the school bus never did and soon the driver, Mr. Bill Stevens, would be at our corner and we would clamber up into the warmth of the big yellow bus. Since we were the last stop, the next challenge was to get turned around on country roads made even narrower by snow drifts, then we were back up the hill and on our way to school for the day—or part of it.

On stormy days the classroom always was a skittish place with kids fidgeting in their seats, attention focused more on the windows than the blackboards. Finally the intercom would buzz and the principal's voice would begin to announce which group of bus kids were being sent home. Then it was back into those layers of clothes and out into the bus. Since town kids often stayed in school for the whole day I actually remember feeling rather deprived by these early dismissals. But, by the time we actually got home, our farm house really did feel like a haven after the bus trip back through the snowstorm and the walk in from the corner. I was fortunate that my brother, being a little older, always broke the path and there also were times, when the winds were particularly frigid, when he would tie my scarf over my entire face and lead me home.

Some days only those bus routes on the country roads would be cancelled but our school would be open. When this happened we thought ourselves fortunate to have the option of following a winter trail out in a different direction to a highway that was kept plowed in all except the most severe of blizzards. I believe that the first time I ever spoke back to a teacher was in the fourth grade when I was criticized in class for missing school the day before when my mother had allowed my brother to take the trail out but had decided that I should stay home for the day.

My determination to not be defeated by being snowbound also was reinforced by my parents. I don't believe my father ever missed a day of work because of the weather. My mother, even though she was not native to this snowy place, also battled the snow tenaciously. Our family dentist told the story for years of how she once appeared for her appointment carrying a pair of snowshoes.

But in spite of, or maybe partly because of, all these efforts to maintain normality, there was no greater feeling as a kid than those when the announcement came that the schools were closed for the day. Freedom. Release from responsibility. Relaxation. I don't sup-

Stirring It Up!

pose kids feel a whole lot differently about it today and I don't think adults ever really get over the excitement of a good blizzard either. In fact the feeling of that primary classroom waiting for the announcement that school would close is not that different than the atmosphere in the local video shops and grocery stores when people are stocking up for a stormy weekend. It's as if we all like to be reminded on occasion that the affairs of people still can be overridden by Mother Nature.

I suppose what kids do when snowed in differs somewhat today since we didn't have computers and VCRs and I was almost in high school by the time we had a television. But certain activities don't seem to change—reading, playing board games, napping, and, of course, snacking. Whatever else we might do on a snow day one thing was always included. We made fudge. My mother started us on this ritual but by the time I was twelve, I was the fudge maker in the family. The funny thing about it was that I almost never succeeded in actually producing anything that resembled the firm creamy substance most people think of as fudge. It always started off with great promise—the smell of the melted chocolate, the sugar added in slowly, the constant stirring. But somehow I never could seem to get the stuff to stiffen. I would keep dropping little dabs in cups of cold water to see if it would form the ball that meant the candy was ready to be poured into a pan. I would beat that syrup as hard as I could. Other family members would take their turns beating the stuff but somehow we usually had to settle for it getting semi-hard and call the end result "spoon fudge." Still, next snow day I would try again.

One treat that always turned out was *toasted Cheerios*. While my mother maintained that she had gotten this recipe off of a Cheerio box, the fact that I've never met anyone else who ever heard of this combination made me think for years that she really must have made it up. Then, just a couple of years ago I actually did find a Cheerio box with the recipe printed on the side panel. I didn't bother clipping it out since it's really a very simple procedure. All you do is melt about a third of a stick of butter in a small sauce pan, add a couple cups of Cheerios, mix it up, add lots of salt and eat the stuff right out of the pan with your fingers. At least that's the way we did it, and it tastes better this way. If you use a spoon the whole recipe is destroyed.

Recently I was having lunch with a group that included folks who had grown up in a number of different Upper Peninsula towns, including Ahmeek, Kingsford, Crystal Falls, Iron River, and Gladstone, one who had been raised on the Iron Range in Minnesota (we accepted without question her experiences with snow and cold), and a few transplants from "down below" who claimed that they too had experienced snow days (we were polite). The conversation turned to childhood memories about food and snow days and one food experience that it seemed almost everyone associated with being snowed in, was the making and eating of a fried bologna sandwich. It seems that this might be the first cooking experience for many snow country kids. Each family, however, had its own twist on this dish. One woman, who says she still does it this way in spite of her husband's askance looks, fries up the meat in a pan with ketchup. One of the men said that in his family the bologna was fried crisp and then put on homemade toasted bread with brown mustard—mustard flavored by horseradish. I remembered the sister of a friend of mine who always burned both the bologna and the toast black and swore this was the only way she liked it. And you thought Toasted Cheerios sounded weird.

But the really vivid memories for everyone were of the baking and cooking that their mothers did during these confinements. One man mentioned big homemade donuts and two of the women stated that it was then that their mothers would make "the best chocolate cake." (My mother did, and still does, make the "best chocolate cake," and I too remember how intoxicating the smell of it could be on a winter day.)

However, as I remember from long ago, it seemed that the aroma of the soups and stews created a barrier against the wind chill perhaps as important as the real protection of the house and its fires. Recalled as favorite soups were chicken and rice, sometimes with tomatoes; vegetable beef started with a big beef bone; and, by almost anyone who grew up anywhere in the Upper Peninsula, pea soup with ham. Our Iron River participant remembered a dumpling and salami soup made by her Italian grandmother. I remember the smell of Finnish fish and potato soup cooking on a winter day, but I fear it was with no pleasure. I was an adult before I came to appreciate this ethnic tradition and then not until I traveled in Finland and ate the dish there. My favorite soup from childhood was a simple pot of ham and navy beans to which I added ketchup. (Heck, having confessed to toasted Cheerios what's a little ketchup?)

Other hardy winter dishes also were remembered. A couple of folks said that a favorite winter meal in their family was macaroni mixed with tomatoes. No butter. No cheese. Just macaroni and canned tomatoes. We talked about polenta—that traditional Italian porridge made out of corn meal. The woman with the Italian grandmother remembered it served in what was called red gravy in her family—a rich tomato sauce—and sometimes, especially in the winter, rabbit meat was added. A man whose mother was of Croatian descent also remembered polenta served under braised pork or beef with peas and another man whose family was Irish-American said he had never heard of polenta but his family ate fried corn meal mush served under rabbit meat in a traditional brown gravy. Now everyone didn't necessarily like all the dishes he or she remembered but the memories of them cheered and warmed us.

Different families and different traditions, but the lesson is that food really does have the power to challenge the physical and emotional chills of winter. And so our recommendation to you as we all struggle through this cold and snowy winter of 1996 is to stock up on the ingredients of your childhood winter meals and when the temperatures drop and the drifts are high, re-create some memories.

In case you have misplaced your own family recipes (or perhaps know that you like remembering what your family ate but your own tastes have developed to a somewhat more sophisticated palate), I asked my own family cook and regular writer of this column, Don Curto, to dig in his files and find a few hardy winter dishes that are guaranteed to get you through until spring. They're cheaper than a plane ticket to Arizona. Then—because it really is "the best"—I added my mother's chocolate cake recipe. Happy New Year.

Meat and Beans Dressed Up for Company
Serves 6
2 C. dried pinto, Great Northern or pea beans, picked over, soaked, etc.
3 large onions
3 whole chives
1 bay leaf
11 garlic cloves
1 Tbls. salt
1/2 stick (1/4 C.) unsalted butter
6 Tbls. olive oil
6 meaty lamb shanks studded with slivers of garlic and rubbed with crumbled dried rosemary and salt to taste
1/4 tsp. crumbled dried rosemary
1-1/4 C. beef broth
1-1/4 C. dry red wine
6 slices lean bacon
1/2 C. dried bread crumbs

In a kettle combine the (soaked) beans with water to cover by 1 inch and add 1 of the onions stuck with the whole cloves, the bay leaf, eight of the garlic cloves and the salt. Boil the mixture for five minutes and simmer it, covered, for twenty-five to thirty minutes, or until the beans are just tender.

In a heavy skillet heat three tablespoons of the oil over moderately high heat until the foam subsides. In the fat, brown the lamb shanks and season them with salt and pepper. Add the rosemary, the broth and the wine.

Bring the liquid to a boil and simmer the shanks, covered, for one hour.

In another skillet, cook the remaining two onions, sliced thin, in the remaining three tablespoons of oil over moderate heat, stirring, until they are browned lightly. Cook them, covered, until they are softened and season with salt and pepper.

Drain the beans, reserving the liquid. Put half the beans in an 8-quart casserole and top them with the onions and the remaining three cloves of garlic, chopped fine.

Transfer the shanks to the casserole. Top them with the remaining beans and pour the lamb braising liquid over the mixture. If there is not enough liquid to cover the beans, add some of the reserved bean cooking liquid.

Top the mixture with the bacon and cook it, uncovered, in the middle of a preheated 350 degree F. oven for one hour.

Sprinkle the top of the mixture with the bread crumbs. Dot it with remaining one tablespoon of butter, cut into bits. Bake the mixture, uncovered for twenty to twenty-five minutes, or until the bread crumbs are golden.

Royal Soup

Serves 4 to 6

A chicken soup you could serve to any members of royalty that happen to drop in this winter.

1 C. chicken breast meat, cooked and chopped.
2 egg yolks
1/2 tsp. salt
1/8 tsp. freshly grated nutmeg
4 C. rich chicken broth
4 Tbls. Parmesan cheese

In a small bowl combine chopped chicken breast, egg yolks, salt and nutmeg; mix well. Bring broth to a boil. Remove from stove.

Add chicken mixture and cheese. Stir vigorously for two to three minutes.

Terry's Chocolate Cake
Combine in one bowl:

1-1/2 C. sugar
2/3 C. shortening
2-1/2 C flour
2 tsp. baking soda
1 tsp. salt
1 C buttermilk
1/2 C. cold coffee (or water)
1 tsp. vanilla
1/2 C. cocoa
2 eggs

Bake at 350 degrees F. for forty-five minutes. Frost with your favorite chocolate or peanut butter frosting.

—January 1996

In the olden days

My Uncle John Tobin will be ninety years old next April and his memory remains exact and packed with detail. He gardens, fishes and drives to town; except for some slowness in gait, he could be mistaken for a man twenty-five years younger. He's my mother's brother and represents the Irish-French-Indian side of my family, my Italian father's culture always was grounded in the Copper Country of Calumet-Laurium and he never really did accept the Irish side, nor did they accept him. I spent several hours with John Tobin recently, talking about Christmas and Marquette in the period of 1910 to 1914, just prior to World War I.

Marquette was a decidedly different place then. First it was poor; second it was quiet; third it was small. There were no automobiles in the streets in the winter; there were no snowplows, except for the streetcar line which ran from Baraga up Front to Hewitt, west to Third and north to Fair, around the corner and down Presque Isle to the car barns (now storage places) at Hawley. In the summer, the cars went across the Dead River to the Island.

At Christmas time there was no easy transportation in or out of

Marquette except for the railroad. If you lived in Marquette, you were here for the winter. Your local transportation was most likely your feet, perhaps attatched to skis or snowshoes as required. Some were lucky to have horses to draw a sled, which sometimes slipped into the "canyon" created by plowing the tracks while the rest of the street had several feet of packed snow.

The noise we know today, even in so-called quiet periods, didn't exist then. There were no aircraft flying over, no autos, few trucks, no stereos blaring from cars. My uncle says that between Christmas and New Year's Day, the first below zero temperatures usually were reached and then you "could hear the sound of a man's boots on the snow a mile away." Other sounds were sleigh bells; at night these signaled a doctor making a house call. John Tobin lived at the corner of Crescent and Third and thus the rattle of the streetcars was a part of the environment and not really noise. One of the other sounds he recalls is young men on the way home in the dark, whistling popular songs of the period.

He remembers those Christmas times as being for children. He says that they were poor, but didn't know it. Kids got mittens, socks, scarves and a few toys which were made of wood or of cast iron. Boys got railroad cars of iron, soldiers, spinning tops; girls got ball and jacks and dolls. There was no common use of aluminum and there were no plastics.

My uncle's favorite toys in memory were "Billy Bounce," a fat doll modeled after a comic strip character whose skill apparently was only his ability to bounce, and The Piper, a figure about eight inches tall, dressed like a military piper which when pressed in some spot would clap two cymbals together.

Food, then and now, was at the center of the celebration. On personal reflection, I would guess that food was probably more important to the Christmas season than it is now because there were fewer distractions to the food then. Now we have so much food that its importance is diminished.

Stirring It Up!

Food came from LaBonte's, a former fine grocer at the corner of Prospect and Third, and from Delf's, a grocer and wonderful vegetable store on Washington Street next to Doncker's, which also supplied fine candles, shoppers' lunches and a wonderful gathering place. He remembers Warner's Market on Front Street (Later Rose's Mens Wear) where the Lighthouse Bookstore is now. He recalls a large heat radiator in Warner's where one could put cold, wet mittens to dry. Delf's had a fine mist of water sprayed over the vegetable racks, just like the "modern" stores of today. Delf's displayed large glass-covered enameled tubs filled with shucked oysters on the sidewalk in front of the store.

Except for the holidays, meals were built around pea soup and cornbread, rice soup, potato soups of great variety and "spaghetti with tomato sauce." Meats, after about November, were salted meats; fresh meat largely was gone. I put the "spaghetti" dish in quotes because it was not spaghetti as we think of it today, but a soupy American idea of what Italian spaghetti was. My father railed against this meat, but to no avail.

For the holidays, my grandmother made mincemeat and French New Year's meat pies. She made apple pies and cranberry sauce and bread, lots of bread. She proudly used only "Franklin Mills Entire Wheat Flour." Even at the holiday season, my grandfather, when asked what he wished for lunch would say, "a piece of bread and a cup of tea," except when strawberry shortcake was on the menu. Then he was likely to eat it all. My grandfather was the turkey carver back then (even I can recall a little of this operation) and he was surgically neat and precise, as one would expect an accountant to be.

My uncle remembers Santa Claus of period as being tall, a little skinny and not at all the joyful fat man he is now. (With fat being cast in such an unfavorable light now, perhaps we'll go back to this.)

The Christmas tree of that time always was the balsam because at the end of the branches the needles form a cross, thus it was the "Christian tree." Lights were candles carefully placed on branches, carefully lit and never out of sight. John Tobin remembers a neighbor (the house that is now adjacent to Vango's on Third Street) during this period who dared to have painted electric lights on his tree. "We thought of them as really ugly," he said, not graceful and elegant as candles are. So, things change.

Kids got up early as they do now and most under-the-tree gifts were practical items of clothes, etc. But the stocking contained the small toys, some raisins and always was topped with an orange, a real treat at that time. Church service in that Catholic family was high mass on Christmas morning—the Christmas Eve midnight mass, if it was invented, had not yet come to Marquette. Turkey was, of course, the center of the holiday meal. Immediate family from the neighborhood always attended Christmas dinner. But the big holiday for the Irish-French family was New Year's Day. The all-meat French pie (still available locally at Lawry's) "toutcaire" was consumed with a lot of wine and brandy. There was an old saying, my uncle claims, that accounted for a next-day hangover, "Them toutcaire's too rich."

Christmas of today certainly is different; my uncle's early Christmases seem spare, almost bare. Yet, without knowing the future holidays, the presents of that time must have been fun for children. It is difficult to visualize a Marquette city so small and slow-moving that the big community Christmas tree was set up in the middle of Washington Street in front of city hall. The city shopping center comprised of stores on Washington, Front and Third streets and everything was available on foot. North Third Street, he said, ended at what is now Magnetic; forest began where Jack's IGA is now. He attended Normal School reached via a woods path angling from Third to where the University is now. Normal School later became John D. Pierce.

Was the celebration of Christmas better then than today's raucous times? Probably not, but it wasn't worse either. Just different. The ability to remember one's life pageant seems to me to be a great gift, an almost magical talent. I hope that your Christmas,

Stirring It Up!

which will at some future time, become an "Olden Christmas" in your life, is a good one.

• • •

Does Santa have his workshop, house, elves and train his reindeer at the North Pole? Of course not. First of all, the North Pole is cold, I mean cold! Secondly, the North Pole infrastructure is poor to nonexistent—no roads, no living quarters, poor communications, etc. I had not planned to release the location Santa Claus uses for training his reindeer and planning his worldwide forays, but at this time of the year, I feel a compulsion to reorder the myth about the North Pole and Santa Claus.

What I am about to reveal to you I saw with my own eyes and as a journalist I certainly would not deal with anything but the facts. Think about the North Pole as you know it and realize that the whole idea of Santa living there is preposterous.

Now, if you believe that there isn't a Santa Claus who monitors children's behavior, makes and distributes toys and games, quit reading right now, because you won't believe what follows either.

Santa lives, works and trains his help in Finland. At the Arctic Circle, well north of Helsinki is the city of Rovaniemi. Tourists visit this entry city to the Far North, thinking that Ultimate North, the Arctic Circle, has been reached. But this only is the barest beginning of the North and few people rarely go beyond it—to Vikajarvi, Sodankyla or due north to Ivalo and beyond where the Laps (Sami) live and reindeer stream across the highway, stopping infrequent traffic.

Santa security does not give me the liberty to reveal the exact location of what I am about to describe, but suffice it to say that it is far north of Rovaniemi but somewhat south of Karigasniemi. Driving a van, descending from a hill on Route 4, heading north to Norway, our goal of that summer of 1988, I suddenly saw before me that the paved two-lane road I was driving on became a great, wide, concrete-paved four-mile-long landing strip. Measured in auto-lane language, it must have been ten lanes wide. It first appeared that this huge strip, deep inside the Arctic Circle, on a piece of flat plateau, barren of trees and most other growth, was an international emergency landing strip for over-the-Pole air flights, possibly for the wide-ranging patrolling bombers of the West during the Cold War.

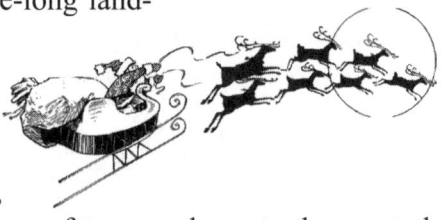

It first appeared that way, I admit. But, while it was a nice cover story, it was far too simple, this easy answer. Then I noticed, almost at the other end of the strip, through an early morning haze what appeared to be a sled with reindeer pulling it. The rig rose into the sky, made a graceful turn and proceeded to make a series of touch-and-go landings. Ah! I thought. Of course, the ideal place for Santa to practice and train new replacement reindeer teams. Santa may live forever, but reindeer don't and new units need practice. As we sped down the strip, I heard the faint tinkling of bells and the sled pulled by reindeer made one last turn into the sun's light and I lost sight. At the end of the runway were simple antennae, and I realized that Santa's workshops and his entire worldwide communication system were underground for economy of both building and heating.

I understand this kind of culture better than most because of a particularly close relationship my historical family has with this area. If you'll look at a detailed map of Finland and find Route 952, you also will note that not far from the shores of Riipijarvi is the small village of Kaarto. This, of course, is a historical translation of the family name into Finnish.

It was here that my ancestor, Charles P., on his way via the Pole route to race Marco Polo to China, was lured by a beautiful Finnish woman to the domestic life and had a town named after him, though the spelling was altered over the centuries. Legend has it that he raised reindeer for milk, meat and clothing. But he specialized in deer that were particularily great leapers, almost seeming to fly through the air. Later in life, he formed a partnership with Henry T. Claus, an entrepreneur from the Continent who had the improbable nickname of "Santa Baby." Later the baby part was dropped.

And that's the story. Believe it.

—December 1995

My father and food

When I was a child, along about this time each year my father would go to Anderson Fish House near the ore dock in Marquette and bring home a fine Lake Superior trout that probably weighed in at about seven or eight pounds, dressed. (Trout in those days were more formal and frequently dressed in tails.) The trout was washed under running water, carefully cleaned inside and filled with large pieces of sweet onion. As I recall, a couple of whole cloves were dropped in with the onion. The fish then was closed with strings and sewn neatly along the belly incision line.

Thus prepared, the fish was placed in a large roasting pan on a spread of butter. Lemon juice was squeezed over the resting trout. It was baked until done, but not until falling apart. The fish was taken from the roaster, the onions and the backbone carefully removed and it then was cut into serving size pieces.

The fish was served without the skin, and with boiled small potatoes, sometimes tossed with butter and dill, sometimes roasted and sometimes mashed with garlic and chopped green onion tops. I'm sure we had a vegetable, too. I also have a vague memory that the broth in the roasting pan was strained through cheesecloth and used as a base for a potato soup. I am not a fan of fish broth, so I'm not sure of just how this was used.

This all comes about because Ms. Tikkanen questioned me recently regarding what kind of food I remember my father preparing. I was shocked at how few of the specifics I can recall. Bothered by this, I have been casting my mind back in search of memories; the problem is, that's pretty far back now. It is indeed strange that the second of two persons who propelled my journey into food interest beyond mere survival and nutrition (my grandmother Tobin was the other) left so few recipes for me. Of course, my father cooked without recipes, mostly, and what he left me was not prescription, but philosophy.

Charlie Curto

I don't know how most men remember their fathers so many years later, but I have long thought of my dad as the unmeanest man I ever knew. He had a restraint on his temper that I have come to realize was most unusual. "Fools get angry," he said. He never struck me and only God knows why not. I realized my good fortune even then because I saw enough cuffing around in the families of my neighbors. He spent much time and energy trying to make my life better than he perceived his to be. Yet, except for a marriage that probably should have been terminated without waiting for death to do it, he had a life that provided him a job which he always enjoyed. He had many friends and co-workers who admired his skill as a locomotive fireman and engineer. Don't read more into this than it deserves. My father was not a saint; he had his share of prejudices, too.

But I have strayed from food.

Recreating my father's food philosophy brings about something like this: food is nutrition, one cannot be healthy without good food, but food is a gift, too. Each ingredient should be considered for its effect upon the others; food preparation, while it may have some undertones of science, is an art; a beautifully prepared and presented dish may not rank in art value with a Monet, but if you can't see the value of the meal you are not likely to see the full value of the painting either. He wouldn't have put it this way, but he behaved so. What is wrong with junk food is not so much its lack of nutritional value, but its lack of art, of intimate care in its construction. This is the stuff that will destroy the soul.

My father carefully cared for everything. When beefsteak tomatoes first came out of Rutger's University he got some plants and raised them with loving care. When he was "on the road," I did the watering using a mixture of rainwater, city water and sheep manure all kept warm in two fifty-five-gallon drums. I considered this a terrible chore until the *tomatoes* ripened into magnificent red, heavy globes of heavenly texture and taste. We ate them whole, sun-warmed off the vine, with a little salt, or cut thick, on top of a big slice of Bermuda onion on buttered fresh whole-wheat bread from the Marquette Baking Company, just up Third Street. For a number of years my father's beefsteak tomatoes won top prizes at the Marquette County Fair.

Another development worked out by my father will give further evidence of his artful care with ingredients. His family background was Northern Italy and polenta was a regular feature in our home. (One correctly may call polenta "corn meal mush" if one wishes, just as one correctly may call a New York strip steak a piece of steer muscle. One may.) If the polenta was to be used as a cereal or to be fried and served with maple syrup, he prepared it with a little bit of salt; but if it was to be used as a starch to carry a chicken and tomato sauce for example, he cooked the polenta in a one-half strength chicken broth. Full strength, he reasoned, would dominate the polenta. Now, many years later one reads of creative city chefs recommending this method. Try it yourself, polenta ceases to be corn meal mush.

Charlie Curto was an outstanding cook and he refined recipes that have stood the test of time in my taste. He got tired of too much tomato sauce, he said. So, he took the Chicken Cacciatore, or hunters' chicken, which always has tomato sauce and changed it to a dish with almost no tomato—about a tablespoon of tomato paste—which recipe I have reproduced in the past.

In later years, he visited me when I was working in the East. I introduced him to the publisher of the paper I worked for, a man from a nationally known family with a heritage of public service. Jokingly, I mentioned that this man's father had left him millions and the family tradition of politics. His grandfather and his father had been senators and governors and that he, my publisher friend, had been lieutenant governor and was sure to be a senator in the family tradition to which he was bound. (He didn't make it.) "Well," my father said, "I will leave you something vastly more valuable than money and tradition. You don't have to do any of those things. You can go where you want, do what you want—I leave you freedom." Not bad for a guy who graduated from fifth grade in Calumet, Michigan.

• • •

Caught up in the lamprey craze

I am certain that I would have done nothing with this topic, which surfaced first with a Duluth dateline in one of our local papers, if Loretta Acocks had not telephoned me one evening recently. Even then, I might have made only a quick, passing reference. But, not one to miss an opening, she brought me several pieces of cooked lamprey, some recipes, some background from Minnesota publications about the decades-long attempt to find a way to persuade people to eat the creatures and a challenge to taste what she and Dr. James Acocks had prepared.

Stirring It Up!

Best of all, the Acocks provided the story of an adventure and even though I've edited it considerably for space reasons, it's their story and I don't think the flavor of it has been lost. I did taste the cooked lamprey and after you read Dr. Acocks' piece, I'll tell you what I think.

When Loretta returned from a meeting recently she said, "Guess what I brought home." She invited me out to the garage and by gosh she had four sea lamprey swimming around in a plastic bag. They were about fifteen- to eighteen-inches long and very much alive. When I asked what we were going to do with them, she said, "I have a recipe and we are going to eat them."

Apparently she had been bugging Mike Twohey of the Fish & Wildlife Service to get her some lamprey to eat in the belief that since we eat most things that come from the sea, and a lamprey is eaten in Portugal where it sells for twenty-five dollars a pound, it was worth trying. The lamprey that Twohey got for her came from eighty feet underwater in Lake Huron that morning. There were some directions for cooking from a man in Duluth who had gotten them from Portugal. They said "kill the lamprey and immerse in hot water." There were no specifics on how one kills the slippery, slimy creatures. So we used barbeque tongs. I grapsed the head firmly and Loretta stuck an ice pick through the head a couple of times and then we held the head under very hot water for a minute or two.

Next step—cut about five inches off the tail end. Then Loretta slit the belly with a razor blade and then we used scissors to cut the belly wall until we could identify the bladder and liver. The lamprey's belly was absolutely packed with thousands and thousands of eggs. The lamprey was divided just behind the gall bladder, taking care not to injure the bladder. The rest of the body sectioned in two pieces.

This operation reminded me of pre-medical school days when we dissected sharks in Anatomy 101.

We began butchering the first lamprey. We thought we'd do just one, but by now we had water and blood over the entire sink and windows, so we decided to tackle the other three.

The original instructions called for the collection of the blood to be incorporated into a sauce and suggested the meat be marinated from two to five hours. They thought the meat to be chewy when cooked. We decided that the blood sauce would be eliminated. It just did not sound very good at the time. Loretta thought that marinating overnight would be in order and we did. The next day the lamprey were put in a hot skillet with olive oil, garlic, onions and mushrooms. They were turned frequently as they browned. The heat was lowered and the pan covered and they were allowed to simmer for an hour.

And with a salute to each other, we had our first bite of sea lamprey and, by gosh, it was good. Tender as liver and a slight taste like liver, but really a taste of its own.

At first, the idea of eating them did not appeal to me, but when I realized that anything cooked in olive oil, garlic, onions and mushrooms would taste good, I thought it worth a try, at least. Now I have to tell you that the sea lamprey is indeed edible, that to me it tasted not like liver, but like mushrooms crossed with snails. I can easily visualize a sauce of lamprey in olive oil, garlic, red pepper flakes, some capers, a generous dash of fresh lemon juice and roasted red peppers over pasta with a side salad and some crusty bread.

As an ending, I note how relationships ebb and flow as time passes. I had planned the piece about my father without knowing anything about the lamprey story to come from Dr. Acocks. So, here we are, writing about Charlie Curto and Dr. Acocks. I recall that the last relationship between these two was when Dr. Acocks signed my father's death certificate in August 1973.

—July 1996

Finland, food and I

In company with my mostly Finnish wife, off to take part in a women's conference, I first went to Finland in August of 1987, then again in June the next year. Perhaps this makes me one of the best Finland-traveled Americans with no Finnish blood and prior to my first visit, very little interest in Finland. I was born and raised in the Upper Peninsula and Finns were not portrayed always in a favorable light those days. They were thought of in the culture that I knew as people with an incomprehensible and unlearnable language, with churches of gloom and doom (though my own Catholic church of the time was hardly a place of sunshine and good cheer) and with food almost as bad as lutefisk.

It is true that only the Finns repaid their War Debt and, later, beat the hell out of the Soviets (those "dirty Commies") in the first Winter War. The newsreel film of that war showed fighting men dressed all in white, on skis, skimming over the frozen land. It was stirring and raised the level of approval of Finns.

So there I was in 1987, thinking, for the first time, of the country of Finland as something real. What did I know about it?—

Nothing from the literature; nothing from their economics; a little of their geography, only because I am a map nut; almost nothing from their history; from their music only a little Sibelius, some polkas and folk music to which I am musically deaf (my personal loss), little of the food, colored by a second-generation Finn friend who said (never having been to Finland), "Oh, you'll really hate the floury cream sauces, the fish...everything is white; there are no spices." My mental "picture" of Finland was created by the "Finland Calling" television show, which, like all specialized portrayals, skews the picture. It shows mostly elderly local Finns returning, touring, watching folk dances, looking at statues and other features, all to a background of polkas. I realize that it is not the purpose of that show to give a balanced picture of Finland.

What a shock to go to Finland and almost immediately discover what a seriously incorrect "picture" one has been carrying around. First, Finland is not a small country; it is big, almost as large as France. It just doesn't have very many people—only about half as many as Michigan. In 1987, Finland is modern, bustling, rich, well-fed, organized, a happy mix of urban modern business hustle with side-by-side rustic and rural. Finland is clean, clean, clean. It is tidy, too, and its organized transportation and highway system made travel simply easy. It has a housing problem—not enough of it—but works at it.

On the 1987 trip of over two weeks, we covered much of southern and eastern Finland by train and auto; in 1988, we drove from Helsinki north to the top of Finland, into Norway and east to the Barents Sea, one of the few spots in the world where one can drive a car north of seventy degrees latitude on paved roads. On that same trip, we drove to the east and down again through the lake country, then west through Porvoo (a truly lovely city, what a great cafe/pastry shop in the old section) and back to Helsinki.

There is nothing backward or third-rate about Finland. Our cities should look so good. There are no slums, there seems to be little great wealth. There is, of course, a certain kind of sameness as this is a nation of great uniformity.

Stirring It Up!

So, you might ask, how's the food? Well, it's not New York or Paris, but is sure beats Wales. The variety, especially at breakfast, and its artful presentation are my lasting impressions. Like all regions, food depends on resource. Eskimos don't have the variety of the Romans; Finns don't have the variety of New Yorkers. Although for Finland, modern transportation and communications have increased the resource and as with the rest of the developed world, we get to look and eat more and more alike.

Here, in no particular order are some of the foods prepared for us in Finland. Some of these are available at Finnish tables in the U.P.; not many locals, however, prepare the elaborate displays we saw in Finland.

At an early evening reception at a publishing company in Helsinki, we are served from a long table with wines set at each end and, between, a display of crackers, breads, prize-winning Finland cheeses, fruits and berries which might have been just ordinary if it weren't for the beautiful china, the fine linens and the graceful arrangement. This is something we note during both visits—the integration of food, linen, china into art.

At a later supper at a restaurant in the city, we find a place hugely affected by America—one menu page devoted entirely to pasta dishes, one to pizza dishes and one to hamburgers. (Pizza is reported to be the second-selling fast food, behind the ubiquitous tart-like piirakkaa.) And the food was good; the ice cream, made there, was wonderful and the concoctions were like ours. The atmosphere was informal, noisy. It was crowded. We visited this place several times. It could have been moved to any American city and fitted perfectly.

In addition to the U.S. influence in food, we saw the obvious influence in music, rock is everywhere; clothing, with distinctive English printing on sweatshirts, and there's very little difference in appearance between American women and Finnish women, in both dress and hairstyle. If anything, the Finnish women, in large cities, are better dressed. In addition to rock music, there's a lot of jazz and classical on the radio. I heard very little polka. Our hostess in

Kuopio for our first visit got quite angry with me when I suggested, half in jest, that I had expected to hear little but polka in Finland. She preferred classical and jazz.

I had an unusual luncheon at a home for the elderly which provided nursing care, attached to a hospital in Kuopio, a university town. The menu: carrot and pineapple salad; beet, onion and apple salad; cheese, lettuce, red pepper, cucumber and pickle salad; cucumber, fruit dressing, onion, pickled tomatoes; sliced ripe tomatoes; a fish salad and the main menu course, salmon and potato soup/stew—Kalakeitto.

Don and Pat's first trip to Finland, 1987

I have notes that in Kuopio we took our host family at their request to dinner at a restaurant called The Steak House, but other than a note that Pat had "salmon and fried potatoes" there is nothing to indicate if there was steak.

In Kuopio I rent a car, and with luck, get a Honda Civic, almost new with little wiper blades on the headlamps. Before we leave, I go to a bakery I discovered in a mall-like line of stores on the edge of the town square and ordered a Kalakukko for the next morning, planned as lunch on the road as we head east toward the lake country and the Soviet Union.

I will let Beatrice Ojakangas, author of *The Finnish Cookbook*, first published in 1964, and probably the most used by Finns in America, tell you what Kalakukko is:

Fish in a Crust

"This is one of the most identifiably Finnish traditional foods. It is made of bony fish cooked in a heavy rye crust for several hours at a low heat. The tiny bones of the fish become soft enough to eat. Slice Kalakukko to serve it, and add to the menu parsley buttered

Stirring It Up!

new potatoes, cucumbers, and tomatoes for a true Finnish meal. The authentic version for the crust calls for only rye flour and not yeast. However, for American tastes, I have revised the crust slightly. The flavor is still the same, but the crust is lighter and easier to chew."

The Kalakukko I got in Kuopio was made with the "authentic crust" and the baker there said it was cooked overnight, for many hours at low heat. We drove east in the rain and ate our Kalakukko near Joinsuu, capital of Karelia, in a park, beside a blue lake. The fish was good, the crust was armorplate.

While in Finland I tried to pick out my favorite new word for each day and it was the Day of the Kalakukko that I discovered my favorite word for the whole trip: Helleosipula—pickled onions. It rolls so nicely off the tongue. It also is in Joinsuu that I find my favorite restaurant name, Al Capone Pizzarea and Restorante. We did not stop there.

At a resort camp twenty-five to thirty kilometers to the south and east of Llomantse, quite near the Russian border, after a day-long hike through some of the Winter War battle areas, I had one of the best meals of either visit to Finland: a salad of Chinese cabbage, cucumbers, tomatoes, a large rainbow trout from the nearby lake, baked brown outside, moist inside, smothered in fried onions. The baked potatoes were served with a cream sauce thick with wild mushroom, homemade bread and locally churned butter were on the table. There also was a plate of hard cheeses and some head cheese. Dessert was a crepe filled with wild berry preserves.

Later, after a sauna, we are served coffee, sweet rolls and dishes of blueberries frozen earlier in the summer. Our journal records that we slept well that night.

Our breakfast before departure was porridge, thick cream, bread, head cheese, pickled Baltic herring. On our way south, we stopped for lunch food at a grocery store and from its in-store bakery we bought piirakkaas, which proved to us that Finland's in-store bakeries do not produce any better stuff than ours.

It is in Imatra, a steel town, that we have a fine meal in Buttenhoff, a restaurant over a store in the business area. This one is Russian-German-Austrian-Finnish, with a manager who speaks fine English. The appetizer is smoked salmon with chopped hard-cooked egg and minced onion. Our salad is half fruit and half vegetables. Pat has her first meal of reindeer pot served in three small pottery dishes, one of reindeer meat in its own gravy, one of mashed potatoes and one of lingonberries. I have Wienerschnitzel, a massive veal steak, covering a large dinner plate. The owner assures me that is the way it is served in Vienna.

It probably is worth recording the number of food items on the breakfast buffet at the Hotelli Vuoksenhovi in Imatra: porridge with cream, little fried wieners, four kinds of bread, two sliced cheeses, two kinds of cold cuts, pickled herring, sliced cucumbers (absolutely everywhere in Finland), tomatoes, two kinds of crackers, eggs (both four- and eight-minutes), oranges, apples, peaches and plums, caviar plate, butter, margarine, jam, yogurt, juice, milk, coffee and tea. And don't forget the Rice Krispies and Corn Flakes, made by you know whom.

The best meal of the trip, though, was in Helsinki, the night before we left for home. It certainly was one of the most elegant restaurants in town, the Konig, which had a definite European cuisine, I ate a very lightly smoked salmon (just enough to give a slight smoke taste, but not enough to cook) which was then poached and served with a traditional saboyan sauce, boiled new dilled potatoes and fresh pea pods. This could be a New York or Brussels meal.

So, as you think about FinnFest, what kind of food-country is Finland? Remarkable, cosmopolitan, universal. Not much beef, little chicken, much fish. Preparation, combinations, presentations, all artfully Finnish. It is a full, rounded culture and certainly ranks with the best.

—August 1996

Stirring It Up!

From the present to the past—and back again

Well, Pat and Don are off again—and this time the first of several columns about a trip will be written before the journey begins. This is a different adventure—we are going to Italy. We already have visited Finland (twice!) to check out Pat's ethnic heritage. On my part, I never recall any strong desire to visit Italy. During my adolescence, Italy and its leaders were hardly heroes to the world. I grew up with a lot of Italian-style food, but to me this was U.S.-oriented, not Italy-oriented. In the past twenty years, Italy has been rejuvenated; most certainly its food is elevated to the level of the best French dishes. In some cases, its "simplicity" has been lauded almost beyond belief. So now we go to find out.

There is an interesting, wandering timeline leading up to this journey. My story about it begins long ago in Calumet where two brothers, Peter and Anthony Bronzo married two of my father's sisters early in this century. Peter's wife was killed in the Italian Hall tragedy, but her infant daughter was saved. As was probably more common than now, another sister, Mae, married Peter to care for the child. The Bronzo brothers, first Peter, then Anthony, moved to Flint, where they prospered.

Peter "farmed" (I think he mostly bought and sold land on the outskirts of the growing city), made wine by importing a railroad carload of grapes from California each year, took good care of Mae and "saved" child and ate great meals. He also specialized in taking us children on rides in his pony cart when we visited.

He did keep a couple milk cows and Sunday breakfast always included a huge bowl of hot milk, sugar and coffee, laced with a liquor for the adults, whipped to a tall froth and ladled into huge warmed cups. This was accompanied by a tender, sweet bread of some kind. Sunday dinner came after church and I remember at least two kinds of pasta, beef or veal, chicken or turkey, garden vegetables, salads, wine, milk, shouting children, adults all talking at once, mostly in Italian. Laughter, bragging, a few lies, more bragging and laughter. Then naps.

Tony and Ann, on the other side of town, kept a restaurant (Italians and food, eh?) across the street from the Buick plant in Flint. They lived in a modern house not far from the restaurant. They had one daughter, Gloria, with whom I was "in love," right up to our freshmen year in college, mine at the University of Michigan and hers at Michigan State. I "hitched" rides there to see her. But soon I found someone in Ann Arbor to be "in love" with. We kept in touch for many years but finally drifted apart.

(There's another story to be told sometime about that restaurant in Flint near the Buick plant and the famous sit-down strike.)

But, back to the trip's timeline: In the late 1920s, the Bronzo brothers, plus various relatives, felt rich enough to take a long visit to Italy, to the family roots. The trip was by ship, of course, and not trusting transportation in Italy and to show their new-found wealth I suppose, they also shipped a new Buick car with them.

I guess they must have had a good time. When they returned, they urged my father, over and over again to go to Italy. Then came the Depression, loss of work and income, then the War, etc. Always there were either things needing to be done or there was not enough money to make the trip. Always my father wanted to visit Italy, not to see relatives as I remember, but just to see "the old country."

He never made it. Age and sickness spoiled that dream. So, now I go, partly for him, mostly for me. I have no knowledge of any relatives there, only that the family background always was said to be in the North, not far from Milan. My father, a truly moderate person, not given to violence, or even raising his voice, carried an incredible, to me, prejudice against "Sicilianos," which covered anyone or anything south of Rome. I have no idea where it came from but I recall several embarrassing incidents where it expressed itself. Fortunately for my views of Italy, the prejudice was not genetically transmitted.

The bare outlines of the trip are simple enough. The time was chosen by low airfare offers and the possibility that we could both get free at the same time. The arrival (and departure) city is Milan, again dictated by the special fare airline. So, we go from Marquette to Detroit where we change from Northwest to KLM and fly direct to Amsterdam, change planes quickly, and fly to Milan.

We will spend two days in Milan then take a very fast train to Rome. We selected the direct trip to Rome based on the theory that the weather will be warmer there in March than in the north. I have been checking Rome's temperature in the *N.Y. Times* and daytime temperatures have been in the low 60s, which will feel tropical compared to Marquette. Rome is about the same latitude as New York and Detroit, but the weather seems warmer. We will spend six days in Rome. Friends have given us good contacts in Rome and a hotel much used by Marquette people visiting there.

We plan to take at least one side trip while in Rome, but a little "research" in various travel guides leaves one wondering if the planned trip to Naples (and Pompei) is really worth considering:

"Naples itself is a coalescing of gaiety and sadness. Its inhabitants, the Neapolitans, are expensive, noisy, and vivacious. They are imaginative, superstitious, and (about a third of them) unemployed, either by choice or by circumstance—it's difficult to deter-

mine which. But as a consequence, crime is rampant, so watch your wallets, pocketbooks, cameras and such. To be more concise, don't take anything to Naples that you can't afford to leave there.

"Don't go to Naples in fear of your life; just be cautious. The Neapolitans don't want to harm you; they are only interested in your valuables. They want you to enjoy yourself and come back again—with more valuables..." (from a guidebook about Italian travel).

Does this give you a feeling that you want to rush right off to Naples? Is this crime problem, which is mentioned frequently in most guides, real? Well, I have some cards written by a Marquette seasoned traveler which note, regarding Rome:

"Keep a separate photocopy of all your vital documents, such as a passport. Also take an extra photo or two. Beware of bag snatchers on mopeds. Keep equipment like video-cams disguised. Be especially careful in market areas and on public transportation. Bus #64 from Termini station to the Vatican is noted for pickpockets. Avoid streets east and south of Termini station at night (also the Colosseum area) as they're well known for prostitution and drug peddling. Carry your shoulder bag on the side away from motor traffic to avoid purse snatchers on mopeds."

It seems perfectly clear to me that it is the mopeds which breed crime. And to think that I once thought Detroit and New York were bad.

If we survive these crime waves, we take a train from Rome to Florence where we will spend another five days, Pat in search of art and antiquities, Don in search of food and markets. I hope there to rent a motorcycle (certainly not a crime-causing moped) and cruise the Tuscan hills for a day or

Stirring It Up!

two.

Then it will be on to Bologna, the food capital of the country and to Parma, just north. Parma is the home, of course, of two personal favorite foods, Parmesan cheese and Prosciutto air-dried ham. Then, back to Milan and the trip home. While in Milan, I plan to see da Vinci's *Last Supper*, which is after all, also about food. After twenty days of great Italian education, we will be ready to come back to Marquette and probably pass on a lot of stuff that you really don't care about; it's all part of living.

Lest you think my attitude too cavalier, let it be noted that there are so many things of fascination to be anticipated that I find it hard to know where to start looking. I make slow progress in learning to speak Italian. Even though I have a life-long fascination with words, I seem to learn foreign languages slowly.

But just listen to some of the common words and the names of towns and villages—is this not almost music or poetry?

sonolieto di conoscerla
dove abita
colazione, pranzo, cena
si segga
entri prego
Dicommano
Fiesole
Lamporecchio
Gimignano
Collesalvetti
Scansano and Magliano
Siena, Massa and Grosseto
Arezzo

So grazie for reading and arrivedeci until next month.

—*March 1997*

Stirring It Up!

An early spring in Italy

I am writing this from Florence, Italy, where we have been living in the wonderful Hotel Continental at the north end of the Ponte Vecchio, the famous bridge of jewelers. We are on the edge of the River Arno, on the sixth floor, in a large comfortable room with a view.

I know that this is a food column, but for this time I feel compelled to give you some short takes on first views and opinions of Italy. Food stuff, and we will have volumes of it, will come later. The hotel business office has trusted me enough to let me use their Boxer 14.50 computer, which is in the hotel master's office. I am working with Microsoft Word, with a keyboard somewhat different than ours and all instructions along the top of the screen in Italian, of course. So, not only have I mastered some numbers, some days of the week, greetings, place names, many food items (of course) but enough of the Italian version of the computer to get this ready to fax to *MM*. If you get the impression that I am having fun, you are correct.

First, I want to start with some observations on driving (or walking) in Italian cities—in this case, Rome, Florence, Siena and Milan. Several people in Marquette who have traveled this country in the past cautioned me against driving here. "There is a car for every two people in Italy," one man said and "they're all driven by crazy people." I know that this caution was well intended, but it stems, I think, from a complete lack of understanding of Italy. Probably a genetic defect.

Driving and/or walking the most narrow, crowded, virtually impossible street is not difficult or dangerous if one learns certain laws.

Pat at the Duomo in Milan

Start with some astute observations credited by Barbara Harrison in her fine book, *Italian Days,* to Newton Minow, former head of the Federal Communications Commission. "In Italy under the law everything is permitted, especially that which is prohibited, compared to France where everything is permitted except that which is prohibited, and Germany where everything is prohibited except that which is permitted, and in the Soviet Union of that time where everything is prohibited," an observation now applying more to China than to the new Russia.

So, no matter what the signs say or what you think your "logic" is from stateside driving, be prepared to have the rule broken. For instance, if the sign indicates that a certain street is so narrow that getting a motor scooter down it takes skill and is open only to foot traffic, don't believe it because you might be run over by a taxi. On foot, or in a car, you are a "free agent," not restricted by any silly old law or regulation you might be used to at home. While this might seem dangerous, it actually gives one a tremendous freedom, because along with the "anything goes" rule there is a corollary which translates that all traffic—foot, bicycle, motor scooter, taxi or auto—is equal. Trucks roaring down a narrow street should not be given way to. Do not let taxis and cars stop your foot movement. When it is your time to cross the street, go ahead, step out. Do not, do not, ever give way in the middle of the street to anything. (Police traffic is a little more equal.) There is a fine line of attitude involved here: one does not show someone else who is the boss, but who is equal. See how simple that is. Yesterday I drove in streets, if that is what they should be called, so narrow that it was hard to pass pedestrians in single file. But we all agreed to our mutual "equality" and several miles of this kind of travel went without serious incident.

A friend in Marquette who has visited widely in Europe says that Italian women are the most beautiful in the world. I find that view difficult to argue with, but also I find it socially and politically dangerous when one is keeping company with a non-Italian woman. During this visit, I have justified my careful scrutiny of women in our travel as an effort to discover if my friend is correct. It has been a rewarding study and one, I might add, for which I seem to have a natural ability. My very tentative conclusions (my study is not yet complete) are that Italian women are indeed very beautiful and perhaps they might be among the most beautiful in the world. Their appearance is enhanced by the fact that they all seem to have been turned out by a stylist. Those that catch our eyes, of course, are those with the most eye appeal. Short skirts, silk scarves wrapped stylishly around their neck, beautiful leather shoes, a confident walk, modern hair style, etc. These women are stylish. Either these women copy the Italian designers, or perhaps, the Italian designers get their inspiration from watching the Italian women walk the streets of Milan. But, I remember the women of Helsinki being stylish, too. We do not see many overweight women and conclude that the Mediterranean Diet has caught on here.

A shop near the Continental, along the Arno, is owned by an Italian man who almost thirty years ago married an American woman from Philadelphia who was here as a student. Except for visits, she has not returned to live in the States. Her son and daughter speak both Italian and English; her son is a political science student and her daughter will soon graduate from law school. Then, the mother says, she will apprentice out to a local law firm "who will pay her nothing—there are too many lawyers in this town." Does this sound familiar? She says that in Florence there are about 3,000 American women like her, married to local men. Rarely, she says, does an American man marry an Italian woman and stay here.

We walk the ancient streets of Florence (oh! how we walk and walk!) and hear English spoken frequently; some of it is American English, but a lot is British, too. The attraction is *art*. There is so much art here in paintings and statuary that a kind of "art poisoning" sets in if one doesn't take a break from it. Even the guidebooks make note of this problem. American colleges have capitalized on this interest in education here and of course are now the catalyst for increasing attendance. Last evening when we went to visit David, that incredible sculpture, we stood in line with a pleasantly garrulous couple from Los Angeles who are visiting their student daughter here under the aegis of a Colorado school. My guidebook lists offices in Florence for Dartmouth, Drake, Georgetown, Harvard, Stanford, American International, University of Michigan, University of Wisconsin and Pepperdine.

In contrast, the Philadelphia woman notes that over 50,000 Americans live in Rome. I suppose that many are involved with Vatican work, which seems to permeate the city even though its sovereign land is tiny.

It would be unfair to write a column like this without making special mention of the toilets of Italy. Now, you may think this is a strange observation, but when one moves about as much as we have, toilets become important. Try finding a toilet in New York City when you are just out on a walking trip. With the occasional exception of those in extremely heavy traffic areas, such as museums, train stations, etc., Italy's toilets are incredibly clean and stylish. A stylish toilet, you say? How about marble floors and walls,

Stirring It Up!

An outdoor cafe in Rome

modern fixtures with electronic water control, etc. Go into the tiniest trattoria or little bar (mostly coffee) and ask for a toilet. One almost always is directed in a friendly fashion to a room with wooden doors and clean fixtures. If the floor is not marble, it is ceramic tile, usually so clean that you can see reflections in it. Walls almost always are marble or tile.

This is a Roman Catholic country as you know and churches are everywhere, and I mean everywhere. On this trip we have seen three of the four largest cathedrals (duomos) in the world—the Duomo in Florence, number four, the Duomo in Milan, number three, and St. Peter's in Rome, number one. New York City has the second largest but I'm not sure of its name, except it is not a Catholic church. We spent much time in the Duomo in Milan, climbing stairs to the sometimes precarious walkway among the saints (statues of course) with wonderful views of the city. We went twice to St. Peter's in Rome. Once we got blessed by the Pope, along with 30,000 other people. Here are some very quick, probably temporary opinions of the three massive cathedrals:

St. Peter's—Huge almost beyond belief. Holds 60,000 people. It evoked not, to me a very strange feeling of religious qualities, but an awe at is grandeur, at the wonderful art in every nook and cranny. This church is so large that Marquette's St. Peter's could fit inside with a lot of room left over. However, it seemed to me on both visits to be a more richly jeweled theater than church.

Florence's Duomo—An architectural and an engineering marvel. A building that is more beautiful and impressive on the outside than on the inside.

Milan's Duomo—So large that 40,000 people can fit inside for the service. This church, to me has the "feeling" of a real church, a strong sense of awe takes one in control immediately upon entering. I had the sense that not only was I in an engineering masterpiece, in a great church, but that I was "inside" of a silent prayer, that the whole building was devoted to expressing man's yearning for the certainty of eternal "salvation." But perhaps a hope on such a grand scale is worth the prayer.

I have run out of time and energy for this day. This has been a remarkable trip with only one day of rain in sixteen. More later...

—April 1997

Love and passion in Rome, etc.

Falling in love in Italy is so easy. There is, first, the incredible food. Then there are those women—everywhere—who dress and carry themselves with such elegant confidence; their demeanor says they *know* the mysteries of life. There are the hectic cities such as Milan with its high fashion life and raspy motor scooters, the markets of Rome and Florence with those wonderful meat stores and vegetable stalls; the magnificent churches that seem to dominate so much of Italian life as the centers of art and architecture, and everywhere there are manners and affection and kisses and hand holding. Italians seem to like each other and amazingly they seem to like us and be willing to show it, making us in turn like them. I think that maybe getting older makes falling in love so often so easy and so wonderful. It sure beats the hell out of hate anyway.

I find that expressing myself in Italian food is very difficult. At first and even second glance, it seems that the food is very much like what we read about, what is described in cook books about Italy, what is supposed to come out of the recipes in those books.

We tried some elegant eating places but I think that if one is interested in real Italian food, these places should be avoided; *haute cuisine* has become "continentalized" and if you go into one of these wonderful eating places you will find beautifully prepared food, perhaps a bit esoteric, but in its essence, quite similar whether one is in Rome, Paris, London, Helsinki, New York or Seattle. "Gourmet" cooking and "gourmet" menus are becoming alike. Food elegance and creativity are becoming "standardized," just as autos and dress have become, with the distinctions mainly being cost and show.

We spent most of our food *lira* in the trattorias, those smaller, less costly and less formal eating places. There is a certain commonality to the menu organization: Anitpasti, which may include such features as *Prosciutto Crudo* (Parma ham) or *Antipasto di mare* (assorted fishes) *Gamberi in salsa rosa* (shrimp in rose sauce) then I Primi, the first course, mostly pastas, though it also can be soup. The second course can be La Carne (meat), Il Pesce (fish) along with I Contorni (cheeses) or La Frutta (fresh fruit). Then there is I Dolci E I Gelati (that amazing ice cream among them) and La Caffetteria (coffees and after dinner drinks). Most trattoria, whether small or large, even tiny bucas (caves—tiny restaurants in basements or under bridges) serve pizza which resemble ours mostly in that they, too, are round. The pizza menu frequently also includes calzone, crostini and focaccia.

But my Italian experience, admittedly still limited after three weeks in that wonderful place, says that while the menu organization is fairly common, the number of items in each category varies widely and in almost all cases, the final result of an item with the same name will taste significantly different in each place. A good example is one of my favorite quick pasta dishes, here in Italy, *Spaghetti Puttanesca,* also known as *Spaghetti, Prostitute's Style.* There seems to be no real authority on the origin of the name, but generally it is agreed that the Trastevere dish is simple and quick: olive oil and butter, heated, add some anchovies, garlic and hot pepper flakes, cook very briefly, then add some tomatoes, olives and

Stirring It Up!

capers. Cook for about three minutes, and add the cooked spaghetti, mix, plate, and eat a wonderful meal. Simple. Yet, I never had this dish cooked the same way in any two restaurants—sometimes the olives were whole and merely pitted, sometimes they were sliced, some used small capers, some used large capers, sometimes the peppers were more noticeable than other times, frequently the anchovy or garlic taste was more dominant. The taste variations with such simple ingredients almost seem unlimited. But every variation I had in Italy was good. So, what is the real way to make this dish? Who knows.

Vegetable antipasta is another example of the non-standardization of dishes. In Rome, everywhere we ate, vegetables were featured as the meal's beginning. In Florence and Milan, it didn't seem such a favorite and I never had a really good vegetable antipasta after Rome. I was sorry that I had not known this while I was there because I would have eaten even more than I did. On our first Sunday in Rome, I had this vegetable array: eggplant cooked four ways, zucchini cut in rings, cut lengthwise, sauteed and baked; small onions, sauteed with Parmesan, baby fresh artichoke hearts, pickled onion, fava beans, some small cubes of fritatta. In print, it doesn't read like the taste treasure it was. I guess the point is made. The ingredient list might be the same, but the result is more than just mildly different from trattoria to trattoria. It is impossible to cook a meal and say this is the way it is cooked in Italy. The definition would have to be more precise.

There is another factor in making the translation of Italian food to this country almost impossible—pasta is not the same. Even if the package purchased here says it is made in Italy, it can not be the same formulation eaten by Italians. U.S. law says that all wheat flour must be enriched; Italian law says that wheat flour cannot be altered in any way. Pasta with the same brand name made in Italy for U.S. consumption and Italian consumption cannot even be made in the same factory.

So, if someone or some cookbook says to you, "This is *the way* it is made in Italy" or "This is the *true way*," take that to mean this is the way it is made in one family or in one trattoria, because the same dish probably varies in the house next door.

In Milan, we had a pizza on very thin crust, with only a very little cheese (all mozzarella we had was fresh) and topped with a mountain of chopped rucola (a kind of arugala) some olive oil and salt. This was really a green salad on a pizza crust. It works in Milan, but maybe nowhere else. (It is a matter of record that Pat fell in love with the rucola and would have had it for breakfast on Cheerios had we been able to get the cereal.)

I suppose this is the long way of saying that I'm not presenting any recipes here that I got in Italy. The ingredients there are fresh and tasty; tomatoes, especially. The variety of greens is much larger than we can get, at best, here. (I imagine, though, that California is awash in things that fit the Italian menu.) It seemed to me while I was there that with only a few exceptions, all the cooks in these little restaurants must be some kind of genius. I'm a pretty good cook but when I ate some of the dishes like those I make at home, I was saddened. For instance, at home I sometimes make a very fine stracciatella soup, which, God knows, is simple enough (a rich chicken broth, eggs beaten with Parmesan and basil, a small amount of chopped spinach). This is a very popular soup in Italy and almost every trattoria we visited has it on the menu. So, we tried it several times. I don't know how they did it, but I had to admit theirs, each slightly different from the other, were much better. I'm still saddened by that.

Those beautiful women of Italy fit the pattern I've been talking about here: some of the most elegant women I saw were past youth, had some wrinkles if one got up close, possibly the beginning of pouches beneath their eyes, yet the "recipe" of dress or suit, scarf, makeup, hairstyle, shoes, walk, etc., came out as a beautiful picture where the small imperfections did not mar it. It's all about the quality of ingredients and how one puts them together. So with the food, too.

—May 1997

Stirring It Up!

A love affair, continued... three guys go to Italy

Ted Bogdan, John Godo and I recently set sail, so to speak, on a great adventure to Italy in search of history, beauty and great food. In Rome and Florence and the land between we found everything we sought and more. We added knowledge to our treasures. Ted is a professor in Northern Michigan University's restaurant management program, John is chef at The Italian Place & N.Y. Deli and I am the guide. I am the guide because I already have had a powerful love affair with Rome and I know her features and her personality. I sense her perfect balance. I know her warm colors and her soft light and friendly shadows. I often dream of our romance. Rome holds for me a fascination so intense that piazzas and fountains and churches and statues and markets and streets are engraved in my mind; in my mind the pictures are three dimensional and rich with sound and smell and light. I can hear the sounds of silence, too, looking out the window of my hotel long after midnight toward St. Peter's Basilica when the entire huge city seems asleep and the dome of the church is softly lighted. Rome wrestles with history, the carnage in the Colesseum and with the ghosts who still patter about the Forum on Julius Caesar's important state business, hurrying from ruin to ruin. For thirty centuries Rome has been gathering up the world, keeping the beautiful and discarding most of the ugly.

Three guys in Italy: Ted Bogdan, Don and John Godo

For me, there is untold pleasure in joining the ghosts of history.

We leave from Marquette for Detroit where we board a Northwest Airlines plane for Amsterdam and then a KLM flight to Rome. If you go, don't go this route. Avoid NW Air if you can. (We and countless others are forced to fly this airline because the fares are lowest when we wish to fly.) Aside from the fact that NW is an un-cheery airline with crews that often seem terribly unhappy, the Amsterdam transfer point is to be avoided whenever possible. So-called jet lag is exacerbated by the timing of this flight. Example: Rome is six hours ahead of Eastern Time, so a 7:00 a.m. arrival in Amsterdam is in "body time" 1:00 a.m., an ungodly hour to be awakened and forced into a transfer hike, for that is what transfers in this clean, orderly, sterile airport are. NW to KLM ("sister" airlines) means a long, long walk from one end of the terminal to the other and, to make it worse, some significant part of the meant-to-be-helpful moving walkways always is under repair and you not only need to hike, but you do it beside an unfunctioning walkway. What an unkind insult. The KLM flight to Rome is two hours and arrival time is noon, Rome time or 6:00 a.m. body time. By now your poor body timing system is totally out of tune and it is saying how tired and sleepy it is. Don't give in. Fight it for the day; and soon you'll be back to "normal." Returning to the U.S. one gets "jet advance" and you find yourself wanting to get out of bed about 2:00 a.m. or 3:00 a.m. This is an easy one to fight, though I don't and thus I get a lot of extra work done for the first few days after return.

(Last year some of us took a U.S. Air flight from Philadelphia direct to Rome, arriving there at noon, also, but we had a relatively long "normal" sleep on the plane so it seemed much like an ordinary day and there was very little jet lag on that trip.)

Customs waves us past the checking tables without a peek into our luggage. Our planned transfer vehicle doesn't meet us. We take a small van with three travelers for the thirty-minute drive to the center of Rome and to our hotel, the Quattro Fontane (Four Fountains). If one is interested in learning about the heart of Rome it is vital to understand that almost everything in the city is next-to or not-far-from something of great historical importance. The hotel is on the street named Via della Quattro Fontane and just downhill from that street's intersection with the Via del Quirinale where there are four smallish (beautiful) fountains attached to the corners of the buldings. They date from the time of Sixtus V, (1585-90) who reigned over significant redevelopment of Rome. One fountain represents the Tiber River, the other the Nile, one female figure is Diana and the other goddess Juno. This street crossing is also one of the highest points in Rome. The hotel's situation is excellent for us. We are a very short distance from the Piazza Barbarini, a three-block walk from the Spanish Steps, a pleasant hike to the Trevi Fountain, the Piazza Navona and the Campo dei Fiori market, with its adjoining La Carbonara restaurant, serving from a marvelous display of perfectly roasted vegetables.

Our most important goal is education in the Italian kitchen for both Ted and John, Ted for use in his classes and John at his work. We have a friend in Rome, Ms. Peta Hughes, a Welsh woman who has lived in Italy for about twenty years, speaks Italian and as a former restaurant owner, knows both food and many of the purveyors. She is now a tour director and did a wonderful job for us on the culinary tour of last year. For this trip she made arrangements for us to spend time with the manager and kitchen staff of Ristorante Papa Re. (Re in Italian means king, so the English name for the restaurant is Papa Rex.) We had dinner there our first evening and though we were tired, the experience was rare. Papa Re is a large (400-plus seat) restaurant that is not far from the Vatican and caters to large tour groups, especially Japanese, who apparently love Italian food. Marcello Vullo manages the large operation and is a master of table side food preparation, one of the few places in Italy where I have seen it done. John was invited back the following day to "work" from 9:00 a.m. until 2:00 p.m.

Everywhere in Italy we were welcomed warmly into restaurants and kitchens with no restraints placed upon us. "At Papa Rex, I observed preparation for lunch when a large crowd was expected," John said. "I picked up some good ideas and learned several interesting techniques which will speed things up in the kitchen. Some of the platters contained spinach-filled cannelloni with a tomato-cream sauce, bowtie pasta with zucchini, cream, Parmesan and parsley, veal and turkey scallopini sauteed with zucchini, green pepper, parsley and Parmesan. There also was a spaghetti with tomato, garlic, olive oil and Parmesan.

"Before the lunch rush, the kitchen staff invited me to sit with them for their lunch which consisted of spaghetti with olive oil, anchovies, red pepper and garlic and some veal shanks with tomato, onion, veal liver, garlic, red pepper and parsley. I was made to feel that I was a member of the staff."

While John was training, Ted and I ate at La Carbonara and more than filled up on the roasted vegetables there. Even at the tail end of winter, the Campo dei Fiori market was filled with fruit, vegetables, spices, herbs, mushrooms, seafood; and flowers, oh, the flowers in February. Those of us who rarely see this kind of spread offered for sale are faced with two emotions. One is joy at such sights. One is sadness almost to the point of tears that this is not available to us.

We generally made it a point to eat three or four times each day.

Stirring It Up!

John gets Italian cooking instruction at Ristorante Papa Re in Rome

In Rome we went to several of my tried and true favorites: La Campagna, Cafe de Paris on the Via Veneto for desserts, McDonald's for easily accessible clean toilets, to Gargani, one of the City's great Italian delicatessens near the top of the Via Veneto, to Da Giggetto, a fine place in the old Jewish ghetto.

We tried some new places, too, and with the great help of Peta discovered Gino of Trastevere whose pizza ranks so far above anything I have eaten elsewhere that it is foolish to try comparisons. The owners were kind enough to give me their dough recipe and let us observe their techniques. For snacks during our stay we tried pizza when we could but nothing compared to Gino of Trastevere. We also went to Luigi's (second choice as our first was closed) with Maurizio Cremasco a new friend who speaks excellent English, is a lecturer in foreign affairs and knows much about Italian foods. Maurizio also gave us a recommendation to a trattoria noted for its fish; we enjoyed the best meal we had in Rome. Real estate people say that there are three important considerations when one decides to open a retail business: 1) Location 2) Location 3) Location. Well, Ristorante Sangallo either never heard of that maxim or chose to ignore it. Sangallo's address is Vicolo della Vaccarella, 11. If you can find a taxi driver who can locate that address and also can navigate the exceptionally narrow street, even by Rome's standards, the rewards are worth it. Small, beautifully decorated, with only eight tables, we are reminded more of a home dining room than a restaurant. At 8:00 p.m. we are the only customers and worry just a bit that perhaps we have visited the wrong place. We forgot about dining hours in Rome; by 9:00 p.m. all the tables but one were occupied. The customers are Roman, the men well dressed, the women quite elegant and beautiful. Orders are taken, wine is served, conversation bubbles, the single server, a young woman of great skill and beauty, floats efficiently from table to table, doing the work of two people.

Ted and Don at the Colosseum

The menu had appetizers, a first course with pasta and rice items, as standard, but offers two second courses, one of fish and one of meat. In addition there are three chef's choice menus: one of fish, one of truffles and one of meat. Ted opts for the six-course fish menu, being who he is, John speaks up for the five course truffle menu and I, aware of how favor smiles on me, take the four-course meat menu.

One of the dishes on the seafood menu was turbot, currently in season, baked with a potato crust. A baking dish contains the fish, the potato crust consists of thinly sliced potatoes, strewn on top of the fish, baked and browned. The potato crust keeps the fish fresh and moist. Its presentation is, of course, beautiful. The truffle menu is packed with truffles. High point of the five courses is the rigatoni with lobster and truffle butter. I had a beef filet baked with Gaeta olives. I also had a Parmesan pie with San Daniele ham and balsamic vinegar sauce.

• • •

Stirring It Up!

In order to get to Florence, we took the Eurostar, a very fast train that takes only ninety-six minutes to make the 197-mile trip, station-to-station. In Florence, we splurge on hotels and worked out a pretty good arrangement with the Hotel Continental, a modern place at the north end of the Ponte Vecchio, probably the choicest hotel location in the city.

Virtually all of our great experiences in Florence and Tuscany center around and are directed by Kathy Procissi, a cousin of Marquette's Nheena Weyer Ittner. Kathy has lived in Florence for many years, married to Alberto, a gentleman. She has a friend, Elizabeth Cole Carpentieri, another American married to an Italian, Alfonso. Kathy is from Midland, Michigan and Elizabeth is from Springfield, Ohio. Both, of course, speak Italian and English and are wonderful guides to us.

Florence is different than Rome. That sounds silly, because we could say that New York is different than Pittsburgh, too. But the difference between Florence and Rome is elemental, I think. This distinction would not apply to New York and Pittsburgh. The food is different, sometimes subtly and sometime wildly. The city is wonderfully different, with Florence feeling like a much newer city and the antiquities of Florence don't seem as old as those in Rome. Florence was pretty heavily damaged in World War II it seems and the rebuilding is more noticeable. Florentines seem more staid, more uprightly conservative. But the significant city-to-city difference is in the mix of people on the streets. Florence is smaller and the crowded streets are peopled mostly by tourists with a very heavy proportion of Japanese and other Orientals. The next largest grouping is students. Oh, my God the students...everywhere. So, in a quick and undoubtedly inaccurate definition I think of Florence as one large, beautiful, exciting museum and art gallery with most of the people being viewers. Rome is larger, more diverse and it absorbs these same groups making them far less noticeable on the streets, except at some of the strictly tourist sites.

There are five places I would like to cite in Florence. The first is Kathy and Alberto's "Trattoria," which is their apartment in

Florence. We were invited to a lovely three-hour dinner there on our first night in the city and that is where we met Elizabeth (a Smith College graduate) and her husband, Alfonso, an Italian with a very wry sense of humor. The food at dinner was wonderful, but the real highlights of this meal were the conversation and the people. We now know what it is like to dine with an Italian family at home.

Kathy was responsible for setting up several fine restaurant visits for John and Ted while Elizabeth led John on a complete tour of Florence's very large Central Market, city headquarters for fresh meats, vegetables, flowers and where some prepared foods also are served. Each merchant has his specialty, some feature fish, lamb, some veal, some beef or offal such as tripe, sweet breads, brains, etc.

Not everyone likes tripe, but I do when it prepared so that it doesn't chew like thick rubber bands. Sergio's in Florence, first discovered with Kathy's help on a previous visit, makes a tripe luncheon dish which has been prepared with tomato, onion, oil and a broth, cooked until the tripe is wonderfully tender and the cooking sauce has thickened almost to a paste consistency. With freshly baked bread, even the Tuscan saltless bread, it is a rare lunch treat.

Then there is the Buca dell'Orafo very near our hotel and discovered by Pat and I on our first visit several years ago and a personal favorite. Buca means cave and this is a tiny place, down some fairly steep steps; it is operated by two older men as a personal drama, reenacted each night. Top menu items: Ribollita, a traditional Florentine cabbage soup which contains a few carrots, some potato and some small amount of celery. This all is thickened with bread, making it appear to be primarily a cabbage and bread soup. But it is more. None I have tried anywhere else is as fine as this. The famous la fiorentina, a thick T-bone steak from Chianina beef, grilled very rare over coals, is referred to in Florence merely as bistecca. It appears on almost all menus (in Florence and elsewhere, even in Rome) but the best I have tasted is prepared at the Buca. If you are lucky enough to get there sometime, try it.

Stirring It Up!

Ted smells fish at a market in Rome

Two restaurants in Florence have achieved special status with us because of guidance by the Procissis and the Carpentieris who introduced us to them. Pennello on via Dante Alighieri is located in the same building where Dante lived and wrote. It has been under the same management since 1969 and reflects the continuity of imaginative management. Gino Brogil and Giovanni Nenciolini are the owner/managers and chefs are Fabrizio Straccali, Antonio Bassu and Giovanni Bruno. Both Ted and John spent a morning here, observing and learning. We had a light lunch of ossobuco, polenta with Gorgonzola, risotto with four cheeses and spinach with garlic and oil, a regular Italian menu item. Time did not permit our return for an evening meal.

Antico Fattore, not far away, has been a gathering place for not only food lovers, but for writers and intellectuals. Chef (and now e-mail correspondent) Antonio Ricciardi provides some menu items I have not seen elsewhere in Florence. Our dinner, with all four of our hosts, was full and rich and quite different. First course was papparadele, a wide pasta, with liver, lamb, rosemary, celery, carrots, sage, oil and tomato. Then we were served a second course, traditional for Lent we were told, of baby goat (kid) braised in broth with rosemary, onion, sage and tomato until the braising liquid was thick. This was accompanied by braised, sliced artichokes with onion, garlic, white wine, broth and tomato. Our totally unneeded, but enjoyed, desserts were chestnut fritters with pinenuts and whole chestnuts, apple fritters with a sugar coating and a berry tart of current, strawberries and raspberries. Chef Antonio's menu offers some of the most unusual fare we encountered in Florence: pasta with wild boar sauce, gnocchi with black truffle sauce, sausages with beans, sauteed pigeon with olives, grilled pigeon, rabbit with fried onion rings, brains with fried artichokes, pigeon with onion. Next time I will sample more.

The purpose of this unique trip was learning; we accomplished even more than we had hoped. There is a kind of excitement about going to a strange land, traveling as an adventurer, operating alone. But there is more if one is fortunate enough to have friends in that country who share your interest and excitement. In both Rome and especially in Florence, our friends did that. In Rome, our friend Peta took us by the hand, at least figuratively, and directed us to what we needed.

In Florence we were taken into the family and came as close to feeling as if we were Florentines as three guys from Michigan could. We thank them.

Note: We learned a great deal about Italian foods, about people and places. We would be glad to impart some of this to any reader who cares to contact me. We are not interested in being selfish about what we learned. Our guides, mentors and friends in Italy were not.

—April 1999

Meanderings far away

Some South Pacific Stuff

In September of 1945 I was a still-new Marine second lieutenant on Guam, twelve degrees above the equator, serving uselessly in the twelfth Marines, the artillery battalion for the Second Marine Division—uselessly because the war was just ended and the battalion wasn't firing, even for practice, and my artillery training was minimal, but under the theory that Marines can do anything, I was assigned there. We took long marches up and down the rugged inland part of the island, with heat and humidity competing for the highest mark. We searched for unexploded shells in the impact area of the firing range and marked them for later destruction. At night, we sat in the battalion officers' club talking, singing, smoking, drinking, all the while thinking of women. Some of us had tried, at first, going down the hill when we could get permission to Agana, Guam's largest town. Too many people, too many Army Air Corps guys from the nearby base, not enough women to go around. The club was a South Sea island thatched-roof hut, with a bar built of local material. There was nothing elegant about it. There was a good stock of liquor, lots of beer, a Marine sergeant to bartend and run the operation. For the life of me now I don't recall how we paid for drinks or what they cost at this place. We might have used chits and paid on payday. Who cares, anyway. Our quarters were pyramidal canvas tents with wood floors and side flaps for ventilation. We slept two officers to a tent. Mosquito netting was standard and pity the poor man who under the influence of too much alcohol didn't get his netting secured mosquito-tight. My tent mate was a friend from advanced infantry training at Camp Pendleton in California. He, too, liked Alexanders, a drink made with Mexican Coffee liqueur and cream. We had managed to stash some coffee liqueur in our locker boxes, leaving behind some unnecessary clothes. But, on Guam there was no cream. So, canned milk which we found somewhere filled the bill. Not much of a drink, but, even out of aluminum canteen cups it gave us the feeling that we had not given in to the island culture and we carried some of Los Angeles with us.

The club was lighted with three bare bulbs strung on a wire from one end to the other. These didn't provide much light as the battalion generator was overworked and failed often, but unit regulations set 9:00 p.m. as closing time anyway. Our biggest party, in the short time that I was there, celebrated the daring venture of one of the division recon units which had been unofficially "assigned" to liberate a new jeep from the Army Air Base (which was rich with jeeps while we were poor) get it painted Marine Corps green, register it, and not be caught. I don't think the Army ever discovered its loss.

That night, the lieutenant colonel who was our battalion commander and a great drinker, shut the club down by borrowing the .45 Colt from the bartender (kept to shoot any left-over Japanese who might try to get a drink) to shoot out the three lights. He was able to hit only two of them, and finished a whole clip without hitting the third one. The sober sergeant finished closing by shooting the third bulb at the colonel's order. Such was life in late 1945 on Guam.

Stirring It Up!

• • •

Fun and Excitement in Peking
By early November of 1945 I had left Guam and sailed to China to replace Marines who were returning to the States.

My office in Tientsin, North China, was in a former Buick dealership building in the pre-war American zone, quite close to the Hai River and on a beautifully wide main street. Circumstances and a large amount of just plain good luck had landed me one of the best jobs in China—public information officer for the First Marine Division—a job normally held by a major. Things at the end of the War were not normal and with old-timers having high points for returning to the States jobs were filled with people of lesser rank. I was of the "lessest" rank with only new gold bars.

Of the twelve second lieutenants shipped north from Guam to replace returning veterans, my friend Boyd Compton and I were the luckiest. Ten of the new officers were shipped to platoons guarding railroad bridges in some of the most isolated country in the world. An important rail supply line ran from Tientsin to Chin Wang Tao, 180 miles to the north. Communists (we were ordered to call them "dissidents") disrupted rail service regularly, forcing delays while repairs were made. The bridges were critical and if damaged the most difficult to repair. Marine infantry units were stationed at these bridges. From each of these tightly guarded locations they could send repair crews to fix broken rails. A light observation aircraft flew daily, weather permitting, from Tientsin north to inspect the tracks and radio the nearest platoon if disruption was found. (I made this flight as a passenger/observer and that is another story.)

My friend was assigned as Officer in Charge of the Marine radio station for North China and I got the public information job. I had working with me some of the best, most experienced writers and photographers one could ask for. Bill Camp was chief writer and boss of the editorial section. He was the author of *Skip to My Lou*, a famous and successful novel about the dust bowl migrations of the thirties which unfortunately had been diminished in its success by John Steinbeck's *Grapes of Wrath* published just ahead of Camp's book. Bill was a former newsman in San Francisco who returned there only to die a tragic death soon after. There also was a public information office in Peking, ninety miles away which was under my direction, though the young sergeant in charge there needed almost no direction from me. I can't give his name here because I'm not sure if he is still in Maine. I don't know if there is a statute of limitations for infractions occuring in China in 1946, but I don't want to take a chance on it. Bill could get anything, anytime, from anyone. His most famous acquisition was required because somehow, the editorial section had lost authority to have a power take-off jeep which was required to make wire recordings. Bill was instructed by those in need of the jeep to "acquire" one, have it repainted and get it registered to our section without violating the restriction on our "owning" one. Sometimes a blind eye by the man in charge is better than offering help or getting in the way. I suspect that the Tank Battalion searched almost everywhere for it. We later transported that jeep deep into the interior of Shantung Province where we used it to make recordings of Chinese bandit groups singing battle songs. These groups were allied loosely with the Nationalist forces as mercenaries. Some of these recordings are stashed away safely in some archives in Washington from where the original order to record originated.

 I went to Peking as often as I could arrange it. It was a much more beautiful city and more exciting things were happening there. My sergeant had "acquired" a personal rickshaw driver whom he shared with me when I visited. (In another piece sometime I will write more about that rickshaw driver.)

 It was at a British legation party in the summer of 1946 that I discovered the aphrodisiac power of Fame. In those days, even in postwar Peking, when the British had a party, it was elegant and prop-

Stirring It Up!

er. The old buildings in Peking had been used by the Japanese, but little was damaged. The outstanding feature of the British Legation that I remember was how large the main room was—it truly was a ballroom. We had been planning for participation in the party for many weeks. There were many newspaper and magazine correspondents in the area, especially because meetings were being held between the communists and the nationalists to try to implement a cease fire set up under the auspices of Gen. George C. Marshall. Peking was the center of the Chinese world at this time. And nothing drew newspaper people like a good party. The Marine public relations office provided them with what services it could—transmission help to the States, transportation when possible, access to liquor, etc. Mostly they were a demanding bunch, but some of them were fine.

With the help of my Peking sergeant, I made the acquaintance of a young woman who worked for a civilian U.S. government agency—she was dark haired, tall, slim, elegant looking, spoke English, dressed American and she was not Chinese. It should be pointed out here that "not Chinese" in China, at this time, was the element that made even the plainest American or British or Russian woman, after a while, look like Rita Hayworth. We were surrounded by Chinese, and many of them very beautiful, but while familiarity may not breed contempt, it does tend to breed blindness. For every occidental woman there were thousands of Marines and some Army, too. (Though with Marines around, Army never had a chance.)

I did know, at one time, the name of the beauty, but I have forgotten it. You'll understand if you stick with me now that you have gone this far. I dressed in the best Marine uniform I had—starched and pressed khakis, shined shoes, proper in every respect. I didn't fool myself even then that it was my intellect, personality or looks that made the date happen. It was my position with many things available hard to get elsewhere. But, ever the optimist, I felt sure that this could and would change. We arrived in my personal jeep, were met at the door by British functionaries from the legation and escorted into the building. A crowd. We made an elegant couple, I thought. Heads turned, people whispered to each other. On the edge of the crowd, paying no attention to me but looking long and hard at my date was a very handsome civilian, somewhat older than I. It was John Hersey who had come to China to write an article for *Life* magazine about a village between Tientsin and Peking: "Red Pepper Village." He also was the very famous and successful author of *A Bell for Adono* and the very recent *Hiroshima* about our atom bombing of that Japanese city. My date asked me who he was; I told her. She asked to meet him; I complied. After that I only saw her from a distance. I forgot her name. I never read anything that John Hersey wrote. Now, he's dead and I'm alive. But, I still think he won. That was my love life in Peking in 1946.

—July 2000

A working journey...
and a sentimental one

I have, since I returned from a recent three-day small bakery survey trip to New York, been trying to evoke some of the feeling I had upon this return to Greenwich Village after what amounts to a forty-seven or forty-eight year absence.

In those long-ago-days the Village was my cultural and spiritual base. At first I had almost no money and was looking for a job. Nedicks (once a big chain of hot dog stands) had a breakfast of orange drink, small sugared donut and a cup of coffee for twelve cents. The subway was a dime and walking was free. Early supper was spaghetti at Eddie's Aurora, an Italian restaurant on West Third Street, now a vacant building beside a McDonalds. Supper was fifty cents if I ate before 5:00 p.m. My waiter, a wonderful Corsican who became a friend, took pity on me and often dropped off bread or rolls left on some other diner's table instead of returning them to the kitchen.

I walked the streets of New York, especially those in Greenwich Village and looked into stores and restaurants. I knew all the streets and had some nodding acquaintanceship with Village regulars. I got a job and had some money to visit these places. I walked, mostly because that's how you get to know a city. I found New York friendly and never felt unsafe on the streets.

This time I dropped into New York, a day or two behind the Pope, not knowing how I would feel about the Village, the people and the places. It is dangerous to wait almost fifty years to go back to happy places. I walked this time, too; I never used the subway or rode a cab once. Little is missed when one walks.

The old Village of my youth is contaminated by the aforementioned McDonalds, a Subway and a Taco Bell—their particular flash and garishness grates. But that's it. *The more things change, the more they remain the same.* Streets bear the same names; youth, now as then, is dominant; noise is everywhere; people are everywhere and they flow, they stream, they eddy and swirl into whirlpools in front of markets, sidewalk cafes or around a hotdog vendor. Traffic is thicker, but not much. The noise, the people, movement and horns blend to make a New York symphony.

After all those years, it was like coming home and it was not a disappointment; I felt like I had not been away long. New York people still are friendly and helpful and the streets of Greenwich Village felt particularly comfortable and safe. I stayed with Bill Cox (a Marquette native) and Arthur Levin in a lovely old townhouse, just off Fifth Avenue on a quiet crosstown street. It was just like in the movies, only better. (There was a brief shot of this fine house on a recent episode of TV's "Central Park West" when one of the male characters kisses one of the female characters as she opens the gate and runs into *my* room! Pity I was not there.)

Restaurants, bakeries, pastry shops, flower shops, incredible delicatessens, markets vying with the best in the world. Food, that's what Greenwich Village has in vast abundance—rich, rich, rich. And the richest must be Balducci's. A grocery, market, delicatessen of such compact complexity, of such color, sound and smell that the full, round feel of these vast riches almost is impossible for my meager descriptive talents. My first impression when I walked in on a very busy Saturday afternoon: how awful it must be to be poor amidst such riches; second, how can I move everyone out of this place so I can have the whole market to myself?

It was impossible, of course, in the short time that I had for this visit to see all the food operations that I had hoped. My goal was to see as many small bakery operations and bakery displays as I could find. But I found a lot more and I suppose that the best way for me to give you any kind of understandable word picture is to touch the highlights, warning you in advance that a lot of the enhancing detail will be missing.

• • •

Saturday
I am struck with an early epiphany after only a few block's walk along Sixth Avenue—that Greenwich Village's atmosphere, its "feel" has not changed in almost half a century. I feel at home. Into Jefferson Market first and marvel at the clean, elegant displays of breads, meats and fish.

Then, the green stylish awning of Balducci's comes to view. I am like an iron filing being drawn by a powerful magnet. Suddenly, I'm inside, surrounded by shoppers poking this and that, asking prices, checking quality, asking for a taste, feeling the vegetables. I get to sample some cheese and new figs—just sliced. I talk with John, the manager of the deli part of the store about the problems of stocking and product freshness. Just about everything here is top quality. The bread variety and its display is wonderful. I buy some imported Italian muscat grapes—they are sweet, smell good and taste like wine just about to be made. I note that fresh white truffles from Alba, Italy, are in season and sell for only seventy-five dollars an ounce! (That's $1,200 per pound and I am reminded that in 1976 I imported eight ounces of fresh white truffles from Italy through the Urbani organization at only $550 a pound. At the old Kitchen Table, I pre-sold most of those eight ounces and enjoyed the rest.)

(The section on Balducci's was written several years ago but I leave it in the book because of nostalgia. The Balducci family apparently [*N.Y. Times* stories] got into a fight over who would control what or some such nonsense. As a result of this the store is now out of business and we are deprived of one of the great Italian markets of old Greenwich Village. I thought that Italians were able to settle such matters with more distinction.)

Saturday dinner is at home with unusually good Chinese takeout from a local noodle house.

• • •

Sunday

At my behest, Bill and I walk in the warm morning sun 'way over to 156 Second Avenue to breakfast at the Second Avenue Deli. I get their catalog and start to believe that it is "New York's Finest Since 1954" as says on the cover. Wrong. It's okay, but there's a deli in Marquette that has better corned beef.

The rest of the daylight on Sunday is spent on what I call my Bleeker Street walk, which also includes a lot of streets running off that busy food street. I go to Faicco's Sausage shop, featuring fresh and dried Italian sausage, which makes one hungry person even when he's not hungry. Then to Zito's Bakery, where they have been making wonderful Italian bread for sixty years. (Did I get bread from Zito when I wandered these streets almost fifty years ago?) Now I get a fresh new roll and munch my way further west. I spend my day looking at this and sampling that, wandering for miles of streets. I am reluctant to sit down to lunch because there is too much to see. I almost eat at the Waverly on Sixth Avenue because I am astounded by a menu with over 402 individual items on it. I take a walk through the Tutta Luna Cafe because the window menu proclaims "Smokers Welcomed." I ask about that and a counterman says "Yup" in a New York accent. I finally have a brief lunch at Steak Frites on 16th Street near Union Square. This is a small place and I choose baked eggs over ratatoulli with proscuitto. I admire

Stirring It Up!

the monstrous hamburger and the huge pile of fries near me. Caution prevails and I eat lightly. White table cloths add to the charm of this place and large, heavy stainless flatware is impressive.

A tour around Union Square, historically known for soapbox speeches by rabble-rousers and revolutionaries, now appears gentrified with family gatherings in the Sunday warmth. A bunch of ferocious looking players are having a hockey game on inline skates.

Dinner is at home, prepared by Arthur. A simple, great meal of fresh corn on the cob, a swordfish steak recently residing in the Atlantic, gently broiled, tender and not cooked to death. Then some fresh greens with a vinaigrette. Real Bread from a local bakery. After a decent break, a slice of a fresh fruit tart from Marquet pastry shop. This tart was so beautiful that I suggested it be framed and hung on the wall, not cut into pieces.

Now, that's a meal—my best in the short visit. We watch the Yankees lose to Seattle.

• • •

Monday

I walk up to Twelfth Street, past an apartment house on Fifth Avenue where the fourth floor corner apartment is being used for a movie by Woody Allen and the street is filled with huge trucks involved in lighting the building from outside. I can't figure why he needs all this outside lighting when the sun is shining so brightly. So, I walk past, letting Woody to his movies and I to my food. I am on my way to the Marquet Patisserie, where last night's tart came from. I have a light breakfast of brioche and coffee. Looking at the assorted individual pastries, fruit tarts and cakes, I find it hard to comprehend that these were made individually, by hand, by a human being. I think I might not be able to break apart these creations. I marvel at such artistry.

Now for the long walk down Broadway to Dean & DeLuca. This is a store of such great fame that I want to enter it carefully and not miss anything. (Our Deli in Marquette carries some products from here.) It's big. Very big. It's full of wonderful foods, great bread displays, incredible housewares (copper everywhere), produce, dry goods, meats, cheese and olives. I find one clerk who is very friendly and helpful and two who are pretty snotty. Dean & DeLuca is much bigger than Balducci's but it lacks the warmth, the intimacy and the excitement of that smaller place. Who am I to tell Dean & DeLuca what they need, but they need warmth and elimination of that horrible off-putting "modern" telephone system that even the Martians abandoned last year.

Then it's a slow walk back uptown, through Washington Square to the Gotham Bar and Grill on East Twelfth Street for lunch. And what a great lunch: "Gotham Soup" of the day—rich chicken broth, vegetables and large pieces of lobster meat; fine rolls and butter; then Roasted Monkfish in Lobster broth with leeks, fennel and a new potato. I skip dessert because I have to get to the airport and fly back to Marquette—mission accomplished.

—November 1995

A spicy love affair

I have fallen in love. Again. Will these crazy wild affairs never end!

I have thought much of late of how fortunate I am to be so often enticed into the exciting arms of new and mysterious loves. It must be a terribly gray life without both abiding and new love affairs, to be locked in to a spare and frugal emotional diet. If you wish to remain young you must be in love, over and over again. Sturdy, tested, reliable old loves form life's firm foundations. It is the unexpected, the sudden new perspective, the "oh-my-god-I've-been-blind" realization that opens emotional doors and makes life spicy once more.

In another city, known mostly for its Teutonic dowdiness, on a recent late winter morning, unusually warm and sunny, I found The Spice House. I opened the door and fell promptly and hopelessly in love.

It was partly the sight of the well-planned, spacious interior, but mostly it was the smell. God, what a smell. A symphonic blend of

Fancy China and newly available Saigon cinnamon, hand-mixed curry powders, tellicherry pepper, ground ginger, fennel and dill, marjoram and juniper berries, nutmeg and oregano, sage leaves and saffron, elegant rosemary and sweet thyme—all this in large quantities, in jars and bins, along the brick walls, covering tables and display racks. Everything clashed, like cymbals forecasting sweetness to come—and yet everything blended like oboes and French horns and muted cornets behind the violins.

Let me explain. The city is Milwaukee, famous for beer, heavy German food and equally heavy Harley-Davidson motorcycles. I first was introduced to The Spice House last year by Willard Romantini, restaurant critic for *Milwaukee Magazine*, but that had been a day of almost frantic activity and the shop was crowded and our mission was somehow elsewhere. I was not ready, it seemed. But those smells remained in my memory and I knew I had missed something on that first visit; I had passed by a beauty, catching only a glimpse, and I needed to return.

The Spice House is located in a brick storefront built in 1837 on Old World Third Street in the historic district of downtown Milwaukee. Across the street is Usinger's famous sausage company and the Ambrosia Chocolate Company. Just a few buildings away is Mader's German Restaurant, one of the city's most famous. What a menu mix this block is!

The essence of the shop's decor really is those wonderful smells that welcome you. (Actually, according to co-owner Patty Erd, in days when grinding and packaging is being done, the shop scents escape via the fan in their workroom and the street shares the aroma. For those passing by this is most interesting when pepper is being ground and mysterious attacks of sneezing result.) Decorations are simple—the original brick walls and wooden floors were uncovered in the renovation when the shop moved here from across the street several years ago and provide a perfect backing to the spices displayed in various sizes of glass jars on wooden shelves, in baskets arranged on the floor, or still stored in burlap sacks marked with the mysterious seals of foreign lands. And the

Stirring It Up!

tools of the trade are, indeed, simple—stainless steel scoops, nine different sifting screens, a vibrating sifter, a collection of old-style stone and shearing mills.

By now you want to know why on Earth I'm writing about a shop 190 miles from Marquette. Because it is fascinating and exciting—it's like walking into the middle of a fine painting; everything "belongs," nothing clashes. And it is the nearest, best mine for all the world's spices, not in cans and jars in a supermarket, but in a place where people know of what they speak, where things are done by hand and brain and love of work.

And this applies especially to the young proprietors, Patty and Tom Erd. She is the daughter of the founders, Bill and Ruth Penzey, now semi-retired thirty-eight years after beginning their first shop, living in the suburbs, but still operating a small spice outlet. And they still are the experts, whose great spice knowledge is behind the operation.

The shop's stock is a lesson in world geography. A partial list of their spice treasures tells this story: Adobo seasoning from Mexico; allspice, Jamaica; bay leaves, Turkey; basil (the USA's most-used herb), California; green cardamom, India; cinnamon, Indonesia, China, Ceylon, Sumatra and Vietnam; cloves, Zanzibar; coriander, Morocco; cumin seed, the Middle East; fenugreek, India; nutmeg (with its feathery covering of mace), Grenada; tellicherry black pepper (considered the world's finest), India; saffron (world's most expensive spice), Spain; tumeric, India; and vanilla beans from Madagascar, Mexico and Tahiti.

The Spice House has been presented in many publications: *Milwaukee Journal, Milwaukee Sentinel, Chicago Tribune, Cooks Magazine, Bon Appetit, Martha Stewart's Living, Good Housekeeping,* Long Island *Newsday, San Francisco Chronicle* and the *Denver Post*. The geographical spread proves its fascination.

Furthermore, noted cookbook writers Jane Brody (*N.Y. Times*), Paula Wolfert, Barbara Tropp and John Thorne have referred their readers to the shop for quality spices and herbs. In 1990, Julia

Child, that truly remarkable cook, visited the shop and gave an impromptu cooking lesson. Nationally famous teachers and writers Faye Levy, Richard Sax, Patricia Wells and Jill Prescott have made their pilgrimage to Milwaukee.

I have read much of what has been published. However well-written, most describe the creators, not the creation. Probably the finest kernel about the creators may be in John Thorne's *Outlaw Cook:* "...The difference between the simple knowledge of a craft and its mastery is the difference between ingestion and a very long period of digestion. The Penzeys have so absorbed the spice trade that I suspect the mere whiff of their astonishing Tung Hing cassia cinnamon brings them not only to the ancient groves in China that produce it, but to the intense, perfumed brightness of that piece of bark when it was still sweet of its particular tree."

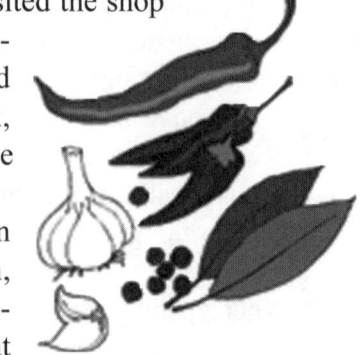

The Penzeys—the people, the working families—are fascinating, but it is their creation that enthralls. Their catalog of available spices, herbs and blends (made by them) contains an occasional recipe and the prices, of course. It also educates, with clear descriptions, and once in a while, with a small essay about a spice—and a little bit more. Witness this catalog entry for pepper:

"*Peppercorns, whole*—Pepper, known as "The King of Spice" or "The Masterpiece" has its vine interwoven throughout history more than any other spice. We consume more black pepper than all the other spices put together. One of the most ancient commodities of trade between the Orient and Europe was pepper, which eventually led to its use as money. During the Middle Ages, one pound of pepper, the equivalent of two week's work for a farmhand, was enough to purchase a scrf. There were times when one pound of pepper was as valuable as one pound of gold and considered a more stable form of exchange on the international market. Returning soldiers received pepper as their share of the bounty. Landlords were only too happy to accept rent payment in pepper instead of money; taxation and bribery worked in the same manner. In 408, when Rome was attacked by Alaric, King of the Visigoths, she was able to spare herself, temporarily, with a ransom including 5,000 pounds of pepper. In the late 1400s, Vasco de Gama discovered a route to the Malabar coast of India, the area where the world's finest pepper grows, enabling Portugal to develop a monopoly of the spice trade which brought the wealth of Alexandria, Genoa and Venice tumbling down. The Dutch eventually were able to drive out the Portugese, but the regions of pepper production had expanded, breaking all monopolies and enabling the ordinary working man to afford pepper also. Although London was the world's nineteenth century spice nucleus, Salem, Massachusetts was the main exporter of Sumatran pepper to the world. This was attributed to good old Yankee ingenuity in shipbuilding; we had developed clipper ships which would swiftly glide around the world with pepper."

Did you know all this before?

So go. Make the pilgrimage. You will be rewarded amply; it is not often that you can walk into the middle of art and merely by being there, become a part of it.

The Spice House, 1031 N. Old World Third St., Milwaukee, WI 53203, (414) 272-0977.

—April 1995

Rituals of spring
with Patricia J. Tikkanen

We were in Milan on Palm Sunday last year. It was the last full day of our vacation—a sunny day but with temperatures somewhat lower than we had come to expect during our long stay in Italy. We ate breakfast in the dining room of our hotel—the Grand Hotel Duomo. As is the custom, breakfast was included in the room cost. Today, ours was an elaborate cold buffet complete with a three-tiered tray of fresh fruit including bananas, kumquats, litchie nuts, oranges, pear and kiwi fruit, next to a platter of thick white slabs of fresh mozzarella alternating with slices of deep red tomato set off with fresh green basil leaves, and surrounded by plates of ham, salami, and prosciutto, rolls and croissants, pitchers of blood-red orange juice (which earlier in our stay we had mistaken from a distance for tomato juice), a bowl of hard-cooked eggs, cartons of yogurt, and what seems to be the universal breakfast food, a selection of cold cereals.

Although it is a very old hotel, the second floor dining room has been redecorated in a modern style—almost Oriental in its simplicity and grace. The floors, of course, are marble but the color of bleached hardwood. The large half-moon windows look out to the side of the cathedral (Duomo) of Milan, from which the hotel draws its name. This is one of the most famous churches in the world because of its vast size—it can seat 40,000—and the 2,300 marble statues that decorate its white marble exterior. Our first day in Italy we had taken the elevator to the roof of the cathedral to wander through its pinnacles and spires, each topped with one of these many statues. We felt as if we were breakfasting with at least a few of these saints from the niches and nooks on the wall across the street from us.

After breakfast we crossed over to the church, the third largest in the world, with the intention of attending the Mass presided over by the Cardinal of Milan. We had visited here several times during both our initial stays in this city and since our return the day before. It's always busy with tourists, pilgrims, and what appears to be regular parishioners. On this morning, however, things in this vast religious cavern were even more bustling than usual. To the left of the main door, folding tables had been set up to accommodate the distribution of olive branches, similar to the palms dispensed on this day in American churches. (We confess to being less than diligent Bible scholars, but after returning home, we did check out several Bibles and found no mention of palms specifically but of "branches" being cut and spread on the road in front of Jesus on his entry to Jerusalem. Not, of course, that we dare to question the correctness of the Italians on such a matter.)

A crowd of several thousand people already had entered the church and taken their seats. The processional was lining up at the rear of the main aisle. Hundreds of tourists still were milling about. There was still a large crowd waiting for their olive branches, which were being dispensed by an elderly man. Pat accepted a few branches and moved over to where she could see the processional pass by. Don, however, had gotten behind a man about the same age as the man working behind the table who refused the branches and unleashed a verbal torrent of displeasure. The man behind the table returned the barrage—complete with shaking fists. This argument continued for several minutes. Fortunately, the cathedral is so large that it merely added to the faint hum of human life that never really stopped as the processional marched in with several dozen alter boys, priests, women dressed with black-lace mantillas covering their heads and finally, the Cardinal, resplendent in his white robes. (We were told later that Milan gossip has him in the running as the next Pope.)

Finally, the branch-giver capitulated and, pulling out a small knife, cut the cord on a fresh bunch of branches and handed several to the once-angry man who politely thanked him for the fresh branches and moved away. This meant, of course, that Don also received the higher-quality olive leaves (which we managed to carefully package and bring back to Marquette for several of our Catholic friends).

This small incident captured much of what we sensed about the character of the Italian people and why not only Italian food is among the very best in the world but why Italian manufactured products from clothes and shoes to glassware and guns are of such high caliber. It seemed to provide support to the cliche that Italians just seem to get more pleasure from living than the rest of the world. Another incident from that day seems to point to this as well.

After Mass, our plan was to visit the most famous of the many "Last Suppers" in Italy—Leonardo da Vinci's fresco in the former Dominican monastery adjoining the Church of Santa Maria delle Grazie. We found it closed and realized that our schedule that day would not allow for a return visit. The site had been closed the first time we tried as well. Somewhat miffed, we wandered instead through the Museo Poldi-Pezzoli, and it was here that we found what we now call our favorite "Last Supper"—a modest painting by Daniele Crespi-Cenacola, a Milanese painter from the early seventeenth century.

Understand that it is not the expression of drama, the use of any revolutionary new techniques, or actually anything to do with the artistic merit of the painting that pleased us—it was the variety in the painting's menu. Laid out on what would appear to be a white linen tablecloth is a meal that includes two kinds of fish, a plate of lemon slices, oysters in the shell, round loaves of brown bread, and an appetizing looking leg of lamb. Passover in the desert may have been spare, but in Italy, the transformed meal is rich with fine foods. We renamed this picture "The Real Italian Last Supper" and went on our way content.

• • •

And a Proposed Easter Feast...
Historically, lamb is the meat most associated with Passover and Easter feasts. Spring lamb is what cooks used to wait for in March and April. In earlier times the first serving of this "spring" lamb involved the superstition of each member of the family making a wish, which was sure to come true. A similar superstition is attatched to eating the first oysters of September, after abstaining for the four months with no "r" in them—May, June, July, August—when it was thought not wise to eat the mollusk. But now young lamb is available all year.

Not all lamb is created equal. As sheep age, the meat's taste becomes stronger and the flesh is more firm. The type of lamb considered most delicate in flavor and tender is baby lamb, also known as milk lamb or hothouse lamb. These animals are produced all year long by controlled breeding. They are slaughtered when they are six to ten weeks old, before weaning. Because it is somewhat difficult to get, this meat is the most expensive.

The largest supply of lamb by far comes from animals born in the spring, which may be as early as January or February in the Southwest. These lambs are slaughtered when they are between six months and one year old. After that age, physiological changes in the animal make the meat taste stronger. Animals slaughtered between one year and twenty months are considered mutton, not lamb. Mutton often gets bad press, but I find it much more flavorful and interesting than lamb. It is almost impossible to get mutton in the U.S. I have found some in a butcher's stall in the West Side Market in Cleveland, and unless I am told differently, there is only

Stirring It Up!

one restaurant in the country serving mutton. That is Keene's Chop House in Manhattan which serves a mutton chop (about one and a half pounds of chop) that can best be described as exquisite. A few years back one of these beautiful things replaced turkey for my New York Thanksgiving Day dinner.

This prejudice against mutton seems to be international. Ten years ago, Pat and I searched the steep hills of Wales and the restaurants of the small towns nestled in their valleys for some mutton from the millions of grazing sheep there. Lamb everywhere. No mutton. Requests by me brought looks of "why is this man asking for something so crude?"

But there is a way to approach the rich, deep flavor of mutton. If you are planning to have a roasted leg of lamb for the holidays this year, let me suggest that you consider a fine recipe taken from James Board and only slightly altered. This is one of Pat's favorite dishes and what I plan to serve to the family in Calumet this Easter.

It requires the use of lamb shanks that can be difficult to get. But I have checked the local stores in Marquette and find that Marquette Meats, near Harvey, carries them regularly (ask for Dave), and Mark in the meat department at Econo Foods will get them for you. Ask for the fore-shanks that are smaller and more tender.

Lamb Shanks with Beans
Serves 6

2 C. dried pinto, Great Northern or pea beans, picked over, soaked, etc.
3 large onions
3 whole cloves
1 bay leaf
11 garlic cloves
1 Tbls. salt
1/2 stick (1/4 C.) unsalted butter
6 Tbls. olive oil
1/4 tsp. crumbled dried rosemary

6 meaty lamb shanks studded with slivers of garlic and rubbed with crumbled dried rosemary and salt to taste
1-1/4 C. beef broth
1-1/4 C. dry red wine
6 slices lean bacon
1/2 C. dried breadcrumbs

In a kettle combine the (soaked) beans with water to cover by one inch and add one of the onions stuck with the whole cloves, the bay leaf, eight of the garlic cloves and the salt. Boil the mixture for five minutes and simmer it, covered, for twenty-five to thirty minutes, or until the beans are just tender.

In a heavy skillet heat three tablespoons of the butter and three tablespoons of the oil over moderately high heat until the foam subsides. In the fat, brown the lamb shanks and season them with salt and pepper. Add the rosemary, the broth and the wine.

Bring the liquid to a boil and simmer the shanks, covered for one hour.

In another skillet cook the remaining two onions, sliced thin, in the remaining three tablespoons of oil over moderate heat, stirring, until they are browned. Then lightly cook them, covered, until they are softened and season them with salt and pepper.

Drain the beans reserving the liquid. Put half the beans in an 8-quart casserole and top them with the onions and the remaining three cloves of garlic, chopped fine.

Transfer the shanks to the casserole; top them with the remaining beans and pour the lamb braising liquid over the mixture. If there is not enough liquid to cover the beans, add some of the reserved bean cooking liquid. Top the mixture with the bacon and cook it, uncovered, in the middle of a preheated 350 degree F. oven for one hour. Sprinkle the top with the breadcrumbs, dot it with the remaining one tablespoon butter, cut into bits and bake the mixture, uncovered for twenty to twenty-five minutes, or until the breadcrumbs are golden.

Precede this meal with a salad of mixed greens or just romaine

Stirring It Up!

with some olive oil and just a touch of lemon juice. Serve the lamb shanks and beans with sauteed carrots. Make a loaf of good bread and enjoy.

Note: Lamb reference help from Meat *by The Lobel Brothers, Hawthorne Books, 1971, and* Lamb *by the editors of Time Life Books, 1981.*

—April 1998

About smuggling, a Cardinal and the Vatican

As I get ready to take off to Italy with other local food lovers, with plans to sample once again the amazing food of that country, a news story in the *New York Times* on August 7 has brought back memories which have been gnawing at my conscience. Stay with me now for the background...

Rev. Alex Sample, Chancellor to the Diocese of Marquette, has arranged a meeting in Rome for us with Edmund Cardinal Szoka, president of the Pontifical Commission for the Vatican City State, one of the highest officials in the Vatican. Cardinal Szoka once occupied the Chancellor's office in Marquette before going on to Gaylord as Bishop, and then to Detroit as Cardinal. Later he was called to Rome to help solve the Vatican Bank's problems. Apparently, the Cardinal misses the U.P. and rarely turns down a chance to meet with visitors from this area.

That said, I now jump to the *N.Y. Times* story. I quote: "Taking aim at outlaw cigar aficionados, federal officials have charged the operators of a high-end restaurant and a private club in Manhattan with selling illicit Cuban cigars to customers...

"...Federal agents armed with search warrants seized hundreds of boxes of cigars from the walk-in humidors of the Patroon restaurant on East 45th Street and Racquet and Tennis Club on Park Avenue. A Federal spokesman put their value at several hundred thousand dollars.

"Robert Gressler, a manager at the men-only Racquet and Tennis Club, and Alex Husbany, manager of the cigar room at Patroon, were arrested and charged with conspiring to violate the Trading With the Enemy Act by buying and selling cigars made in Cuba."

It's that "trading with the enemy" stuff that got me. I know that the statute of limitations applies favorably to me, but, even though the Pearly Gates now actually are a chain-link fence according to a cartoon in *The New Yorker* because of Heaven's security problems, I am a little concerned about visiting with someone as powerful as a Vatican Cardinal without coming clean. But, as we have seen on television recently, confession is difficult.

Many years ago, I was a smoker. Camel straights and Cuban cigars, which in those days were relatively cheap, a dollar and a quarter got a very good one. Regular cigars were only fifteen cents to maybe fifty cents for a good one. The Camel straights, of course, helped me on the way to some serious breathing problems. But in the throes of a powerful nicotine addiction, who knows...or cares?

After President Kennedy cut off trade with Cuba in 1962, Cuban cigars became illegal, even those purchased in third countries which continued to do business with Cuba, such as Canada. This remains true to this day. (Peter Sinton in a *San Francisco Chronicle* story in October of 1996 said that just before Kennedy imposed the ban, he bought 1,100 brandname Cuban cigars for his own use. It was reported that he always kept a box or two around the White House. Of course.) It is well known how effective this embargo has been in removing Castro from leadership. Thirty-six years since the embargo one cannot legally buy a good Cuban cigar. Illegal cigars now sell for eight to twenty-two dollars each, it is reported.

I was in the newspaper business in those days and had some business that took me from time to time to Montreal or sometimes it was a trip concerned only with the business of fishing the lakes far north of Montreal.

On all of the trips after 1962 and up until about 1969 I bought the best Cuban cigars I could find and afford. I suppose that the largest number I purchased to smuggle into the United States was about fifteen or twenty, as prices had risen to over a dollar. I recall a particular trip when I passed through U.S. Customs at Plattsburgh, N.Y. with about a dozen Cuban cigars of the very highest quality. I was very pleased that I had bought such good cigars and that the trip through customs was simple and without incident.

In those days, my friend and childhood schoolmate, Richard "Gin" Nystrom, was director of U.S. Customs for the St. Lawrence Seaway. He and his family lived then in Plattsburgh, N.Y., and on this trip I spent the night with them. The next morning, Gin took me on a fishing trip on Lake Champlain (before that lake had pretensions of becoming a Great Lake). I really wanted to light up a good cigar but recalled that even as a child, Gin was a thorough "straight shooter," much nicer and more polite than the gang of roughnecks he hung out with. And I was aware that customs directors had some powers. So I approached this task somewhat obliquely by asking him: "Gin, just suppose that I got caught smuggling just a few Cuban cigars across the border by your people. What would you do?" He thought for a moment before replying and then said, "Well, we've known each other a long time and I guess if I had the time, I'd visit you in jail." Still a straight shooter.

No Cuban cigars smoked on Lake Champlain that day.

By the way, I would like to note that I did inhale the Camel smoke. But in keeping with a famous denial, I did not inhale the Cuban cigar smoke so I was not infected by any of Castro's revolutionary ideas.

• • •

Places of Distinction

There are times when I don't feel like writing about food. It isn't a matter of being tired of food, but rather the intrusion of other thoughts and observations. For several months, as we have driven around Marquette, my LP (life partner) and I have been noting Marquette sites which seem to us to be places of distinction—projects, private, commercial or public, which have been particularly well done. The places mentioned here certainly are not meant to comprise a complete list of the fine things around town.

Take a close look at the Water Treatment Plant at the foot of Arch Street. What a fine job blending old with new. An addition of distinction to the edge of a residential area which is harmed not at all by this plant; rather it is enhanced.

John Jilbert's building, headquarters of Cellular One and others, replaced a building of absolutely no distinction which burned two years ago. In a stretch of U.S. 41 to the west, which could certainly use something new and attractive, Jilbert's building is a gem. It is worth noting here, too, that Jilbert's newly redesigned grounds around the dairy barn and ice cream parlor are first class. It is apparent that John Jilbert doesn't do things any way except with distinction. There is a new large cow on the roof of an addition to the dairy. Someone asked the other day how that cow "got up there?" Seems pretty simple to me; it was a failed attempt on the part of the cow to jump over the moon.

Often overlooked I suspect, are some of the older buildings downtown which have been maintained carefully and decorated thoughtfully. Getz's Department store has occupied the corner of Spring and Front streets for more than a century, it seems, and the building still seems appropriately up-to-date and fresh these many years later.

Mattson Park remains one of Marquette's great accomplishments. How we could have tolerated for so many years a coal dump of great ugliness seems strange now. (And the coal needed to be trundled through the community via open rail car!)

The Landmark Inn has received so much deserved and undeserved notice this past

Stirring It Up!

year that it should not need more, but regardless of anything said, it is a first-rate job and a real piece of art.

The Marquette County Courthouse was refurbished and refinished years ago, but it remains one of the most distinguished in Michigan. Don't just drive by and look at it; go inside, walk the old corridors, look at the original courtroom with its interesting skylight. The central (main) entrance has a particularly well-done display of John Voelker memorabilia regarding, especially, the *Anatomy of a Murder* movie.

Three museums in a small city: the Historical, the Maritime and the Children's Museum. Each unique. The Historical is the oldest, and the Children's is the newest. These are places of distinction. The transformation of the old, less than beautiful building into the bright Children's Museum was a monumental work, directed by that tiny dynamo, Nheena Ittner.

The Rosewood (former) is a work-in-progress. It is doubtful that even God knows when it will be complete. But it has brought new life to that formerly rundown section of town. It is on its way to becoming a place of distinction.

Even if you don't live in Marquette, it's worth a drive past 808 Champion Street, the home of John and Yvonne Dorais. At this time of year, most flowers are in bloom. The couple does seasonal things with their beautiful white, wide-porched home. These are artists, not just gardeners.

—*September 1998*

Lessons learned in a berry patch

Patricia J. Tikkanen

No food tradition in the Upper Peninsula is perhaps loved more by more of us than berry picking. (And the making of the berry jams, jellies and desserts.) While Native Americans were the first gatherers of this summertime harvest, most immigrant groups to the Peninsula joined in with enthusiasm. Certainly this was true of the Finns who had a tradition of harvesting berries in their homeland. Few Finnish-Americans have not been part of a blueberry picking expedition—though perhaps not all as willingly or with as much enjoyment in the process as I remember. And while many of us may have felt the poetry of the experience even fewer could express it as beautifully as Finnish-American poet Barbara Simila.

I was five the summer I went berry picking alone for the first time. I stood in my mother's kitchen, a plastic water glass that would serve as my first berry "bucket" clutched in my hand, listening to her final instructions. "Only pick those that are really ripe. Leave the green ones for another day. Remember, if you find one or two berries, look around, there probably are more right there. Don't go any further than the rock piles by yourself, and Patsy, don't eat more than you put in your bucket!"

During those years our family lived in a small mining location called Number 4 just north of Calumet in the Keweenaw Peninsula. The name came from the old mine that had produced copper for only a few years leaving behind crumbling sandstone foundations and two large waste rock piles that covered several acres apiece. My older brother and I treated these like our own private mountains and spent hours exploring their crevices and crannies. From their tops, a hundred feet or so high, you had a good view of the Centennial mine shaft a mile to the west where our father worked, while to the north you could see Wolverine village with Copper City just visible beyond.

The rock piles were set perpendicular to each other and formed the north and west boundaries of my berry picking field with our house on the south side and a mostly dry creek bed on the east. It was late June and strawberries were the treasure being sought. Wild strawberries. The small ones were no bigger than peas—the very largest ones about the size of a marble. It takes patience to pick wild strawberries—even a glassfull. But I had patience—or perhaps it was only that sense of timelessness of childhood summers when days seemed to last longer. (A sense I recapture a bit every summer when the sky still is streaked with highlights at 10:30 p.m.)

The morning sun was pouring down over the field but there was enough of a nip in the breeze to make me wonder briefly if my mother had been right when she cautioned against the wearing of shorts for my excursion. But as the sun rose higher and the dew on the grass tickling me dried, I enjoyed the warmth of the sunlight on the backs of my legs as I bent down seeking the small red nuggets.

I developed a pattern. Six berries in the glass, one in the mouth. Unless the berry I had picked turned out to have a little green on it. Those were extra for the mouth. Unless the berry I had picked was a little too ripe to put in the glass. Those were for the mouth, too. Still, the berries in the glass rose higher. It probably helped that I knew that all the berries were for me to eat later in the day in a bowl

Stirring It Up!

with milk and sugar since I still was young enough to be exempt from contributing the results of my labor to those gathered for the jam pot. I filled that glass.

The strawberries of late June and early July are only the first of the berry harvest and in those years it seemed that our family life each summer was organized around the different berry seasons, from the strawberries in June to the blackberries and chokecherries in late August. By the middle of July we were searching out thimbleberries along the railroad and old streetcar tracks near our home and I never tired of hearing how we were one of only a very few places in the world where these bright red beauties grow. We were special. Still, it didn't take me long to learn that it takes a lot of time to fill a bucket with those "special" little things as they disintegrate quickly in the pail into a mushy red lump. Thimbleberries were for jam—most of which was given away to downstate relatives. I'm not sure we ever actually ate any of the stuff ourselves. The same was not true for anything made from raspberries, which would ripen about the same time and quickly became and remain my favorite berry. My mother's raspberry pie was everyone's favorite dessert—still is.

With August came the blueberry season and family excursions to the good big patches farther north on the Peninsula in the sandy soil closer to the shores of Lake Superior. My dad would tell us about how he had come to this same area near Rice Lake as a boy with his father and brothers. Some years they would camp out for a few days with the goal of getting enough berries to "ma" to can to last the large family through the winter. "I never minded picking berries," my dad would say. "You're outside in the fresh air and sunshine. You don't have to think too hard about what you're doing. And you feel like you've really done something when you fill a pail!"

Good thing he didn't mind because it turned out we all did a lot of berry picking for a few years after we moved to my grandfather's farm just south of Calumet. By now it was the late 1950s and Copper Country strawberries had become a big cash crop for farmers in the area. My dad plowed up fields previously used for potatoes or hay and we were in the strawberry business. We kids sat on the back of the strawberry planter feeding the little plants into the machine that stuck them into the ground. We weeded. We plucked off the blossoms the first year a new field had been planted learning that this was necessary for the plants to grow strong and produce berries the next year. And we picked those berries. But for this we were paid: Six cents a quart. On a good day I could pick over twenty quarts. I think I made thirty a few times. I'm still real fast on multiplication if it involves the number six.

I rather liked the whole strawberry picking process: The waking up early on a July morning (with mixed feelings if I could hear rain on the roof above my head since that meant no picking that day—and no earnings), my mom or dad would have driven to town already to pick up a half dozen "pickers" who would join family in the fields. The berries had to be picked, sorted, and delivered to the farmer's association by early afternoon to be put on the train to Chicago, where, we were told, people could just not get enough of our wonderful berries—supposedly the sweetest anywhere. We were assigned rows to pick—no reaching into the row to your right or left even if you saw a particularly beautiful specimen—that was bad form. We picked right into quart baskets fitted in wooden carriers—most held eight quarts. (Forty-eight cents.) I was a pretty good picker. Better than my older brother, Oren, who never really got that enamored of the whole thing. Faster than my cousin Sheila who picked the cleanest more uniformly ripened quarts of anyone in the field. I went for quantity, she for quality. My folks really liked Sheila's berries which required almost no "grading" in the strawberry shack at the edge of the field.

Stirring It Up!

My motivation for money was helped by the arrival, just when the berries were ripening, of the fall catalogs, or "wish books" as the older folks called them—Sears and Roebuck, Montgomery Ward and Speigels. I spent hours pouring over the girls section of those catalogues—adding up various options, calculating and recalculating how much I was likely to end up with that could be used for school clothes. I thought I was very fortunate to have this money to spend and it never really occurred to me that my folks probably would have had to buy me school clothes anyway.

By early afternoon of those berry days we would be finished—picking that is. In fact, for those weeks of the year berries dominated our whole life. My dad delivered the berries while my mom would bring the pickers home before returning home to deal with the tubs of berries culled out from those sold because they were too ripe or too small. Those were saved for our own freezer and jam pot. In those days my mother's hands would be stained red with berry juice for all of July.

I had a whole other job, too. I, with Sheila's help some days, ran the strawberry stand we had on the highway where we sold some of our berries to local folks and tourists passing by. We would open up by mid-afternoon and stay open until all the berries were sold. We were experts at displaying our wares. Every quart had its biggest, best looking berries right on top. And if they all didn't sell quickly we eventually would "refresh" them by pouring them into another quart container and then back into the original to "plump" them up. Sometimes we would take an extra quart and distribute them among those displayed on the front counter to really dress them up. This, however, we were reluctant to do too often as we were paid a small commission on each quart we sold. I still remember, with chagrin, the day some smooth talking man, probably a downstate tourist, talked us into filling a case so full with extra berries on top that we could hardly get it closed—thus losing our commission on those quarts and getting my mom irritated with us for giving away the profits.

The strawberry fields mostly are overgrown on the family farm now though my dad still gets in his share of berry picking each summer in a good sized raspberry patch (no complaints here!) that he has cultivated. My life is busy and I am grateful that from this busyness I earn more than six cents a quart these days. Still, once or twice a summer I make it out berry picking. I like it—being outside in the fresh air and sunshine, the not thinking too hard about anything and the feeling that I've really done something when I've filled a pail. And inevitably I think about my mother's advice, "Only pick those that are really ripe. Leave the green ones for another day. Remember, if you find one or two berries look around, there are probably more right there. Don't go any further than the rock piles by yourself, and Patsy, don't eat more than you put in your bucket!"

—July 1998

Berry Picking

Deep in the summer blueberry marsh
the August sun reaches into the ferry
underbelly of the woodland, bathes
the branches of tag alders and thick
spikes of marsh grasses.
Here where the bittern huddles
in sustained and practiced fright,
jewelled berries spill by moist
handfulls into the bucket I wear
belted at my waist.

I follow worn paths of deer trails
along the fringes of this landscape,
discover the trail of black bear
and her exuberant young;
there are frayed edges of balsam stumps
blueberry bushes torn up by the roots
the occasional pile of seed-laden dung.

I chant the songs of the gatherer
learned from my Finnish father,
ancient runes of old times
sung to keep wild things at bay;
I crouch in the mist
on my haunces, bathed
in a charm of purple juices,
at the heart of this northern life.

—Barbara Simila

(used with permission of the author)

On being an almost purist

The *New York Times* recently printed an article about some of the new restaurants springing up in Philadelphia, a town I remember from my Delaware days as not being much involved in anything later than 1776. It is the following paragraph which directed me to write about more simple things.

The restaurant reviewed here is run by Masaharu Morimoto, best known, it says here, for being on the "Iron Chef" program on the Food Network. (I have seen this show and it could only have originated in Japan, a land not known for great food.) Mr. Morimoto in Philly, has "the ultimate stage set, a cavernous white room on Chestnut Street where plexiglass booths change colors periodically and the sushi bar looks like an altar.

"The food is still a little uneven. But there are winners like a salad of mizuna and unctious salmon toro dressed with a yuzu vinaigrette. Morimoto even makes a production of tofu: a waiter brings a hot bowl filled with soy milk, stirs in a salt reduction and lets it sit seven minutes, until it thickens to the consistency of firm custard, then two sauces are poured over in succession. Crepes

Suzette was never so dramatic."

All of my adult life I have been looking for a salad of mizuna and unctious salmon toro dressed with yuzu vinaigrette. Now that I have found where I can get one, I think God is good to me. However, I would be happier, yet, if Mr. Morimoto would kick that unctious salmon toro around one of his plexiglass booths and pound it on the altar to dispel its unctiousness.

As the big time chefs strive to be ever more imaginative and "creative" they stumble and make fools of themselves. The Chinese may have to eat tofu, certainly a chameleon element, because they have very little access to other proteins but to compare that bowl to the theater of Crepes Suzette forgets that Crepes Suzette are edible.

I suppose it is natural for any decent cook to look for ways to make the job easier; especially commercial cooks where cost of goods and production hours are critical. But...

Take the case of the famous Bolognese meat sauce. It also is known as Ragu. Now you probably think that the ragu label on grocery shelves represents all Italian sauces. Not the case. The Ragu on grocery shelves is okay, but little more than that. It has become a generic term, covering all of the brand sauces, regardless of recipe.

Here is a real Bolognese sauce. The name is from Bologna the famous food city in the Emilia-Romagna region of northern Italy. This is an old recipe from a book dating back to the 1960s, Ada Boni's *Italian Regional Cooking*. I selected this old book specifically because it comes from the days before the huge influx of American touists in Italy and before that cuisine became so popular in the U.S. thus there is a chance that the recipes truly are regional. However, there is a wonderful sauce called Amatriciana, named after a town (Amatrice) to the east and slightly north of Rome which seems to have a slight variation from family to family, almost from house to house. That's regional cooking taken to the extreme. So, beware.

Bolognese Meat Sauce
(Recipe reduced for 6 servings)
6 Tbls. butter
2-1/2 Tbls. olive oil
1 medium onion, finely chopped
1 medium carrot, finely chopped
1 stalk celery, finely chopped
2/3 C. bacon, finely chopped
3/4 C. ground (minced) pork
3/4 C. ground (minced) beef
1/4 C. medium spiced sausage meat
2–3 chicken livers
2/3 C. dry white wine
salt and pepper
4 tsp. tomato paste
About 1-1/2 C. beef stock
4 Tbls. light cream or whole milk

Heat half the butter and all the oil in a deep frying pan. Add the onion, carrot, celery and bacon and fry over a low heat until the vegetables soften and begin to change color. Add the pork, beef, sausage meat and chicken livers and fry these gently until they begin to brown, crumbing with a fork. Moisten with wine and cook until it evaporates, then season to taste with salt and pepper. Dilute the tomato paste with a little stock. Stir this into the sauce, cover and cook slowly, stirring from time to time and gradually adding the rest of the stock.

After the sauce has been cooking for one and one half hours, stir in the cream and continue cooking until reduced. Finally add the remaining butter and stir until melted and thoroughly mixed into the sauce.

About a quarter pound of chopped mushrooms, sauteed in butter and flavored with garlic and finely chopped parsley, may be added to the sauce at the last moment, if liked.

These quantities will make enough sauce for one to one and one half pounds of spaghetti.

• • •

Of all the pasta sauces that I know, the Bolognese is the most complicated and fussy and the longest cooking. Many restaurants cook their tomato sauce for a very long time. I know of one U.P. Italian restaurant that once used a very large sauce pot with a cover which had a paddle attachment powered by a small electric motor for continuous stirring so the sauce does not stick to the bottom of the pot. While many of these concoctions are called ragu or Bolognese, they are in fact tomato sauce, nothing more. Often they become "Italian" because someone puts some ground beef in them and some dried oregano and basil and garlic.

Notice how little tomato this sauce has in it. Pasta sauces do not have to be swimming in tomatoes. Also, if one were of a mind to spoil a good sauce, but still make it passable one could remove the sausage, the pork, the chicken livers and the mushrooms. In addition, most U.S. diners seem to like a sauce quite liquid, sort of like putting some pasta into a tomato soup mix. If one, then, added chopped or pureed tomatoes to this recipe it still would be edible. If one did these things, the sauce would resemble much of what we see around us. But, it would no longer be Bolognese or Ragu sauce, regardless of what we called it. But you can see how easily a purist recipe can be altered because of ingredient cost/availability, the cook's skills and preparation time.

Another wonderful Italian dish has been all but ruined by the preparation time problem: risotto. This famous rice dish cannot be rushed nor can it be held for more than a minute or two. In addition to the time and holding problems, there is the matter of rice. While there are several kinds of rice, all from Italy, which are suitable for risotto, there really is only one major kind generally available outside of the big cities; this is arborio rice from northern Italy. Arborio is best because the grains are fatter, shorter and contain more starch which gives the finished product its creamy texture, a

Stirring It Up!

requirement for great risotto.

Restaurants who want to put this dish on their menu face problems: 1) cooking time, which runs twenty to twenty-five minutes; 2) it takes all the attention of one cook; and 3) it has to be timed to fit the other items going to that particular table because it cannot be held without becoming gooey and gluey. Consequently there are very few places which will submit to this kind of discipline. However, it is now possible (good old human ingenuity) to get a risotto mix which has been par cooked, which contains both onion and garlic flavor, and which can be held for some time because it does not use the high starch Arborio rice. Don't do it because the finished product is truly terrible.

If you see a menu with "risotto" on it and there are no special instructions, such as "made to order" or "you will have to wait" and a note that when the risotto is ready to eat, they will deliver it to your table, whether you are ready or not, it is not risotto. In a place in Milano we were advised that the kitchen had begun preparation of our risotto and approximately how long it would take. We had not quite finished our first course when the waiter brought the risotto, removed our first plates from in front of us and placed the risotto there, with a look that ordered us to begin eating this splendid dish. We did and it was splendid.

There are a lot of good risotto recipes around and it is possible for you to "invent" your own. It is the method which makes the difference. If you can't find a recipe that pleases you, get in touch with me and I'll give one or two or more.

The method is deceptively simple: lightly saute whatever flavorings, usually finely chopped onion, garlic. Add rice, saute rice in the butter/oil flavoring mix until rice starts to brown. Add a stock (chicken or beef as wished; even plain hot water can work) a cup at a time, stir rice constantly as it simmers on low heat. Continue until that liquid is absorbed then add another cup, etc. When the required amount of liquid (two parts liquid to one part rice approximately) has been added and absorbed by the rice, it should be puffed, not mushy, with grains separate and kind of creamy from the starch.

Finish any last minute flavoring, plate and serve at once, with grated cheese if it goes with the dish.

Risotto Milanese (with saffron flavor and color) is probably the most frequently mentioned. Here is an easy to make recipe, quite different, but very tasty.

Risotto with Raisins
Serves 4 to 6
2/3 C. golden raisins, soaked in water or wine
2 cloves garlic
5 Tbls. olive oil
2–3 sprigs flat leafed Italian parsley, finely chopped
2-1/2 C. Arborio rice
about 6 C. simmering chicken stock
3/4 C. grated Parmesan cheese

Drain the raisins and pat them dry with a paper towel. Leave one clove of garlic whole and chop the other very finely. Fry both together in oil with the parsley in a heavy pan. When the whole garlic clove browns, discard it and add the raisins.

Add the rice and stir it thoroughly into the oil and cook for five minutes, stirring gently all the time. Add a cup of boiling stock and when this has been absorbed, add another cup. Continue in this manner until the rice is just tender and still moist. Serve garnished with grated Parmesan.

Enjoy. Life is too short to eat bad food with unhappy people.
—April 2002

The joy of food

Sometimes, when I write about food, I get caught up in my own fascination with it and assume, innocently enough, that everyone thinks of food just about as I do, or an even worse sin of self-righteousness, that they should. Then I speak less for myself than in *Universal Truths*. Here are some personal thoughts about food, with no intention of converting or directing anyone to the *right* way of living and eating. There may be a universal truth or so herein, but that would be coincidental.

We enter, for me, a joyful food time, a period of holidays, one upon the other. Thanksgiving, Hanukkah, Christmas, the New Year, gathering with friends. At U.P. latitudes, where the days grow shorter and the daily temperatures drop alarmingly, I am sustained by Food Art, by the thought of it, by the planning for it. I have many other interests, but I spend less time worrying about the Broad issues, as in the *Hereafter, Eternity,* the *Truth,* than I do about the simple quality of each day.

Understand, I admire people who search for the Universal Truth, the answer to the Mystery of Life. Still, I presently conclude that there is either no Universal Truth and no solution to the Mystery of Life, or, perhaps it is that there are far too many of them. In any case, it seems to me to be a terrible way to spoil a potentially good day. Even supposing that one discovered these great answers; there still remains the problem of living well this day. An important part of that living well involves food, for nourishment of body and spirit.

If one looks upon food primarily as fuel, or as is more popular these days, as medicine, think for a moment of the dreadful problem that approach creates: one takes medicine this day in order to be "healthy" to take medicine the next day and so on to what end? Unending days of medicine?

But evidence that this approach is not working was found in a recent report in the *New York Times* of major study done by the NPD Group in Rosemont, Illinois, reporting that the fastest growing food sales in America are French fries, hamburgers and chicken nuggets! I glean three things from this nugget of information: 1) television advertising is worth every penny a fast food chain pays for it; 2) preachers of food salvation are no more successful than any other salvation preacher; 3) Americans show their independence by doing as they damn well please. While I personally think that French fries, hamburgers and chicken nuggets comprise an unimaginative, salt-taste diet, I am cheered by the disdain the populace has for the Controlling Food Directors.

More examples of the failure of this approach are found in a new book just out titled *Eat Fat* (Richard Klein, Pantheon) which extols the virtues of eating fat, being fat and denounces the diet, skinny look. But this author is not writing about the things that I believe because he carries it too far. Good food does not have to be fat, either. And, clearly, being overweight does affect the health of many people, including apparently the author's mother whose ability to breathe freely was seriously affected by weight. Of course that Mr. Klein can be reckless is demonstrated by his first book *Cigarettes Are Sublime,* about the pleasures and cultural importance of smoking. That these books can become best sellers nation-

Stirring It Up!

ally and get respectful attention is, I think, a sure sign that the diet people have gone too far.

And so what are my personal beliefs? I believe that food is a central part of our lives. That its importance is more than nutrition although the goals of satisfying our souls and the needs of our bodies need not be quite the conflict we are presented by the war between the fast food ads and those Controlling Food Directors. One of the keys is moderation and while I have not been able yet to hold on to that key always, it does present a goal. I believe that one thing that works against this moderation is that when you eat mediocre food in mediocre settings there is tendency to overeat as the only thing you can do to try, unsuccessfully I would note, to satisfy those deeper needs we seek from food. (Note, for example, the current monstrosity being promoted on TV which has *two* quarter pound hamburgers, *three* slices of cheese and *eight* strips of bacon.)

I believe that good and satisfying food need not be prepared elaborately (although there are times when it is satisfying to plan, prepare or partake in such a dish). Good things often are simple. A small example for you—take the lowly rutabaga, peel, trim, cut up, cook in a small amount of water, drain, mash with butter, some sherry, a bit of ground ginger. Serve warm, garnished with some cilantro. Perhaps more sophisticated than what we remember from U.P. Sunday dinners at grandmas but the idea is the same—good, nutritious food prepared to taste good.

I believe that variety in diet is desirable both from a nutrition viewpoint and that it contributes to the sense of wellbeing we seek. We are helped here by modern transportation methods that have made it possible for me to have, even in this agriculturally barren region of the U.P., a wonderfully varied diet of foods with sublime taste if I but learn to purchase properly, to prepare in an artful fashion and to eat with respect for the food. I find that even broccoli tastes better in December when I think about the transportation intricacies which got it from California to my table in snowy Marquette, fresh and crisp.

I believe that how you eat is almost as important as what we eat.

Some eating rules I try to follow: Eat at least two meals a day sitting at a table. Eat at least one of those meals with a family member or friend, with a table set as well as possible with china, good flatware, nice glasses. *No television.* Spend at least forty-five minutes at the table. Talk about nothing controversial. Be aware of the source of food, how it was prepared and its taste subtleties.

And so, while trying hard not to be one of those co-dependent, controlling food people who look with despair upon food trends or who wish that everyone would eat to my standards of "healthy," I leave you at year's end with my own formula. Recognize that our relationship with food is truly complex and that more than grams of fiber and fat are involved in the choices we make. Learn to meet those needs not by self-deprivation but by caring about the ingredients and the preparation of what we eat and the setting where we eat.

Happy holidays, wherever you are.

• • •

(The recipes which follow are simple, yet different. The cucumber dill soup is very tasty; the braised chicken is a great meal which holds well for the next-day use; the sesame cornish hens is another, mostly successful attempt to make these strange culinary creatures interesting; the venison chili speaks for itself; and the braised Brussels sprouts dish will amaze you—it truly is good.)

Braised Brussels Sprouts in Cream
(This may be the only recipe, which was taken from a 1987 New York Times *magazine, making Brussels sprouts palatable.)*
2 C. heavy cream
1-1/2 lbs. Brussels sprouts
1 tsp. finely minced fresh ginger
1 tsp. finely minced garlic
freshly grated nutmeg to taste
salt and white pepper, if needed, to taste

Put the cream in a heavy saucepan over medium-low heat. Bring to boil and cook at a slow but steady boil until the cream is reduced by one-third and thick and yellow.

Meanwhile, rinse and trim the Brussels sprouts. Cut each into quarters and grate or process in food processor until the sprouts are the consistency of cole slaw, but not too fine. If you use a processor, do it in two batches for better control over the results.

When the cream is reduced, add the ginger and garlic and mix well. If you are using fresh nutmeg, grate eight to ten scrapings. If you use prepared nutmeg, shake some in to taste, remembering that nutmeg is potent.

Add the sprouts, turn them in the cream to coat well. Return to medium heat and braise, uncovered for eight to ten minutes. The sprouts should be firm and crisp, but not raw. Check for seasoning, serve at once.

Venison Chili with Apples
(From Waldy Malouf, ex-chef, Hudson River Club, N.Y.; New York Times*)*
1/4 C. vegetable oil
3 medium yellow onions, 1/4-inch dice
2-1/2 lbs. venison stew meat, cut into 1/2-inch dice (can use beef too)
1 small jalapeno pepper, minced
6 Granny Smith apples, peeled, cored and cut into 1/2-inch dice
1/4 C. ground cumin
1 Tbls. chili powder
2 tsp. black pepper
salt to taste
1/4 C. chopped garlic
1 5-ounce can tomato paste
1 28-ounce can whole peeled tomatoes, chopped, juice reserved
1 C. red wine
2 C. chicken broth
grated cheddar cheese and chopped scallions for garnish

In a pot large enough to hold all the ingredients, heat the oil and brown the onions, venison and jalapeno. Add the apples, spices and seasonings and garlic and brown five more minutes.

Add the tomato paste, tomatoes and juice, wine and broth. Bring to boil, lower the heat and simmer, uncovered, for two hours. Adjust the seasonings and serve with grated cheddar and chopped scallions on the side.

Yield: 6 to 8 servings

Sesame Cornish Hens
Servings: 2 hens to serve 4 with other items. 2 hens to serve 2 if that is the only main course.

Split hens by first cutting through back, then through breast from inside. Wash in salt water, dry and place in large bowl, cover with buttermilk for at least four hours.

Lift from bowl, drain but do not wipe. Dip in a mixture of half sesame seeds and half unflavored bread crumbs. Place in shallow baking dish and put in preheated 325 degree F. oven; bake until done, about fifty minutes.

These can be eaten hot, warm or room temperature. Salt and pepper to taste.

Braised Chicken and Vegetables
This is a solid Michigan winter supper, created here, easy to make ahead and pleasing to look at. This recipe is subject to easy variation.
Ingredients: for 4 entree servings

- 6 chicken legs with thighs, separated, trimmed of excess fat; do not skin
- 1 lb. of medium or hot Italian sausage; cooked, cooled, cut in 1/2-inch pieces
- 4 medium baking potatoes, peeled, cut into eighths
- 4 large carrots, peeled, cut into bite size pieces

1 large green pepper cut into bite size pieces
20 small white onions
2 medium firm canned tomatoes
12 peeled cloves of garlic, keep whole
2 bay leaves
salt and pepper
butter as needed
2-3 C. rich chicken broth, can use canned

In a large deep frying pan or braising pan, brown chicken pieces in butter, over medium-high heat; do not burn butter. Remove from pan, set aside. Drain off excess fat, if any.

Place vegetables (except tomatoes) in pan, add bay leaves, pour chicken stock over, raise heat to gently simmer vegetables (including garlic cloves). After fifteen minutes, add the chicken pieces and the cut-up sausage and continue to simmer. Do not submerge either vegetable or chicken in liquid, just enough liquid to almost cover. Remove liquid if necessary, but save it.

Cover pan, continue to bare simmer for forty-five minutes, until all is cooked.

Season to taste. Add tomatoes, partly crush with spoon, just to add some color, not to season with tomato flavor.

Cucumber-Dill Soup
with egg
1 medium cucumber
3 Tbls. butter or margarine
2 tsp. all purpose flour
2/3 C. rich chicken stock (can use canned broth)
1 Tbls. finely chopped dill
salt and pepper
1/4 C. whipping cream
2 hard-cooked eggs

Peel cucumber, chop coarsely. Melt butter in saucepan and stew cucumber gently for four to five minutes. Sprinkle the flour over cucumber, add warm stock.

Simmer for eight to ten minutes, add dill, salt and pepper to taste and stir in the cream.

Place a half hard cooked egg in each of four soup plates and spoon the soup over them. Can garnish with more dill.

—December 1996

The perfect day

I know that it might seem a slight overstatement to announce that any day could be perfect, but when I finish describing October 24, 1998 to you, I believe that you'll agree with me. I suppose it's a good idea to give some indications of what makes such a day.

Some requirements: It must be approached with great anticipation. If the day's activities are outside, the weather must be exactly what one hoped for. One's energy and general health must be high. One's companions must be the most compatible for the activities planned. One's spiritual condition must be unusually good, with that special ability to receive all the signals that create an understanding of the mystery of living. But for perfection, all of these conditions must be surpassed.

And so they were.

Our friends, Michael and Geralyn Derry, who live in a nice suburb of Detroit, probably in itself a form of soft Purgatory, have a condominium on a ridge high over Harbor Springs which, while certainly not in Heaven, must seem so after leaving that sad city to the south. I joined Michael there on Friday evening (spouses off on other ventures) for preparation for the next day.

And what a day we anticipated! Each autumn, Wycamp, a club and shooting preserve about forty-five minutes north of Harbor Springs near Bliss and Wycamp Lake, conducts pheasant drives, in the European tradition, which means that hunters are placed in a line of blinds and after the sound of a horn, pheasants are driven toward the blinds for overhead shooting and only very occasionally some side shooting as pheasants fly by.

This Saturday was more than one could hope for at this time of the year, with a cloudless sky and an early morning cool that quickly rose into the mid-sixties. After a drive lined with brown fields and bright autumn trees we arrived at camp where we joined other hunters. I learned after the arrival that this hunt is quite famous around the country. We and another man were the only Michigan residents. Hunters came from Hawaii (special fly-in the day before), Illinois, Kentucky, Tennessee, Pennsylvania and I think New York—all men except for one woman from Chicago. Eighteen in all.

Dress was eclectic. I am not a regular hunter so I have no "uniform." Fortunately I was able to borrow an Orvis shooting jacket from a friend who wears my size and who is a fine hunter. I didn't want to embarrass either myself or Michael by being improperly dressed. I needn't have worried: dress ran from blue jeans, to work pants and jackets to truly elegant British hunting clothes worn by an elderly gentlemen from Kentucky who had an equally elegant double twelve-gauge Purvis shotgun. Even the inelegantly dressed all had elegant shotguns. Priorities, I guess.

The only gun I own is an old, cheap twenty-gauge double, which was old when I bought it second- or third-hand thirty-five years ago. I would have been ashamed to take that gun. But, always to the rescue, Michael had, in addition to his own gun, a new, never-fired Weatherby over/under twelve-gauge. You need to know here that my friend Michael (a Northern Michigan University graduate) is one of those athletes who doesn't do anything poorly. He introduced me to sporting clays, a kind of cross between skeet and real bird hunting, several years ago. And while I am not the worst marksman in the world, I cannot compare with Michael. In sporting clays the best I have ever hit out of fifty is twenty-nine, which is considered pretty good, especially for a newcomer to the sport. Michael regularly shoots forty-five and up.

Armed with my beautiful, borrowed gun (but minus the classy coat as the morning temperature had risen to almost seventy degrees), I joined the other hunters, the dogs and their handlers for the quarter-mile walk to the blinds. This is former farm land, now grown with scrub pines with the blinds arranged along the edge of an old forest of hardwoods. We used nine blinds, two people to a blind. Each set of two blinds was supported by a dog handler with a retriever. They were all Labradors except for one German short hair, who was a very good retriever. It almost was worth the trip just to watch these dogs work—a four-footed ballet.

Some may believe that hunting from a blind while someone drives pheasant toward you is un-sportsmanlike. (A non-hunting friend asked why we don't just shoot the birds in their cages.) Well, political consideration aside, this kind of hunt is deceptively difficult. The blinds are small and the shooter stands no more than five feet behind the front and side walls, sometimes made of logs or evergreen branches and always eighteen inches to two feet taller than the shooter. This means that there are no easy head-on shots and that almost every shot is overhead, either directly or to one side or the other. By this point the pheasant is at full speed (which I am told can be sixty-five mph) and you might be surprised how many birds fly past.

I had been worried about being the one who fired the first shot with the new Weatherby. I thought that with my lack of experience I very well might miss and bring humiliation upon myself, the gun and my friend who let me use this new weapon. Well, as luck would have it, the first pheasant that flew within

HUNTING SEASON

range of our first blind was brought down by the first shot from the new gun. After that start, it was a whole morning of great luck, from one blind to another.

After a fine lunch at tables set up under an open tent we collected our share of cleaned birds and returned to Harbor Springs, tired, hot and with slightly bruised shoulders from the recoil after so many shots. Coffee and a cigar on the deck in the autumn warmth, overlooking the harbor across to Petoskey, followed by a welcomed nap was the intermission between the morning hunting act and the evening part of this perfect day—dinner at Tapawingo, regarded in many reviews as one of Michigan's finest restaurants. (The 1996 Zagat guide said it had the finest food in Michigan.) For this part of the day, it should be said Michael and I were joined by our lovely and charming wives as, of course, no perfect day would be complete without their company.

Tapawingo deserves its reputation for quality, except clearly someone in command is geographically-impaired in a way so often connected to Lower Michigan arrogance, both private and public. (Remember the agency "map" of Michigan that completely eliminated the Upper Peninsula?) A calling card from the Tapawingo identifies it as *"Fine dining in Northwest Michigan."* Tapawingo is in a town named Ellsworth, which is not far from Atwood, closer to Ironton and Norwood and just a long stone's throw from East Jordan and Advance. I can't imagine that that helps you a lot. But one place it is not is in northwest Michigan. Northwest Michigan would be somewhere around Mass City, or perhaps Baraga. Ellsworth, which is south and a little east of Charlevoix, might be described as in northwest Lower Michigan. If one were going to locate it in the most general terms.

Tapawingo is a good example of the restaurant version of the "build it and they will come" rule: cook it well and imaginatively, serve it with class in a beautiful setting and they will come. Tapawingo is hugely successful with reservations at any time of the year difficult to get. But probably it wasn't always that way. It takes a lot of work, dedication to quality and time to have an operation such as this get this successful in the middle of "food nowhere." I am grateful that Michael and Geralyn, who know a classy eatery when they find it, have chosen this place for my birthday dinner.

The surroundings are elegant, but in a casual manner suited to its country location. Gardens surround the entranceway and the interior is modern but warm looking with yellow walls and white trim around the large windows. There are fresh flowers in small wall vases and more on each table.

Menus change daily and prices are high, very high, especially by rural restaurant standards. (Tapawingo's other somewhat slanderous name is "Tap-a-wallet.") When prices are in this range (marking with some of Manhattan's finest and well above those of several fine Rome restaurants I have eaten at) one expects that everything will be perfect, not just the food, but service and surroundings, too. I think it probably takes a truly picky critic to find any fault with this place. But, having earned the reputation, I might as well enjoy it.

The menu is organized with one hors d'oeuvre, seven choices for first dishes, several salads, and six or more principal dishes to choose from. The dessert menu is separate.

The hors d'oeuvre for the evening was smoked salmon on potato pancake with dill. Of the first dishes, our group ordered venison-black bean chili, fennel torte with escargot and country terrine with cumberland sauce. We all ordered the good, although quite ordinary, apple harvest salad and romaine with prosciutto, blue cheese and walnuts. The principal dishes ordered were rosemary-crusted pork tenderloin: pan-roasted pork tenderloin, crusted with fresh rosemary, served with garlic mashed potatoes, vegetables and shallot-green peppercorn sauce—thirty-six dollars; lamb shank with Parmesan potatoes: tender, braised lamb shank gratineed with a mustard crumb crust, served with a natural lamb sauce and diced vegetables, Parmesan mashed potatoes and frico, a crisp cheese wafer—thirty-eight dollars; and beef tenderloin, rossini-style: beef tenderloin medallion, char-grilled and presented with seared foie gras, black truffle sauce, roasted fingerling potatoes and vegetables of the season—forty dollars.

Diners' comments and observations: The hors d'oeuvre was about the size of a silver dollar; it was all too cute. I think if it had been given more time in the kitchen it may have grown into a fully mature hors d'oeuvre. The salad was very good. The venison-black bean chili was first rate and the country terrine wonderful. The fennel torte was again, "cute" and pretentious—a near flop at an additional three dollar charge. The pork tenderloin was undercooked in the new style and very good, but still rare pork was just not to the diner's satisfaction. The lamb shank (which I tasted also) was "the shank of all shanks." Wonderful. The beef tenderloin was "tender, huge, properly cooked and topped with the most wonderful foie gras." (My spouse won't let me properly describe the fingerling potatoes that came with this item but I can say that if you were walking your dog you might pick them up with a scooper.) Desserts were all good with the raspberry creme brule receiving the most applause.

Service was pleasant and professional except for the server's two assistants who were young and appeared to have been untrained. They reached across diners' faces, poured coffee across the table, and generally intruded, interfering with what otherwise was a most pleasant experience.

In ending, I think that Tapawingo deserves all of the many accolades thrown at it. The food is more than first rate and the dining comfort level is very high.

—December 1998

Life's riches

I begin this piece on Sunday, June 22, the first day of summer in Marquette; it is sunny with a blue sky and high, broken clouds, seventy-five degrees, a tiny warm wind, and it virtually is silent in the south part of the city. My black Labrador, Kate, searches the shallow water of our pond, bringing up a rock, a water-logged piece of pine and some floating birch bark. As a Lab does, she successfully eats it all, except for the new rock, but gives that a second try anyway.

The lawn has been cut and smells like summer, the beautiful birches bend slightly in the warm wind, and only the smallest sound comes from the leaves. Down the pond further, a sharp-edged kingfisher dives into the shallow water and takes his Sunday snack to a tree; blackbirds with their glowing metallic-blue breast skim the water, from edge to edge.

Kate and I are alone—all the other homes are silent. She, disappointed that I won't throw a stick or go in the water with her, comes out, shakes, and plops on the grass beside me.

This week I have been to funeral homes twice; once to help bury a fifty-four-year-old friend who should not have died so young, and once to pay my respects to a man who died at eighty-five and to let his family know how much I liked him As I get older, the interior of funeral homes becomes more familiar.

Today, I can't help but think a totally inconsequential thought: one of the troubles with dying is that one misses so much. Today, with Kate beside me in the sun, I realize how rich in life I am.

● ● ●

A Treasure Found
Over the past twenty-five years or so, a new richness in available recipes of world foods has become available; no longer do we rely on grandmother's recipe for the foods of Ireland, or for the foods of France or whatever country our relatives came from. Travel and the attendant publication of a dizzying array of cookbooks has spread once-local food knowledge throughout the world, ours for the opening a book. Some of us read cookbooks—or books on food—with just as much excitement as others read a mystery story. I am one of those people. It seems that just about all of the original research work on the foods of Europe has been done, and many of the new books out are little more than rehash of better stuff done earlier.

Recently I discovered a book that breaks some new ground in an exciting way. The book is *Cucina Paradiso: The Heavenly Food of Sicily* by Simon & Schuster in 1992. As you can see, the book is not a newly published one, but somehow I missed it in 1992.

This book is a treasure because not only does it explore the Arab influence upon the island of Sicily, but does it convincingly and understandably in its presentation of some interesting recipes. Sicilian food, as well as its culture, has gotten "bad press" over the years, at least until recently. Everything is not "tomato" and all Sicilians are not part of the Mafia.

(I have recorded earlier about my father, whose family's Italian background was from northern Italy, and his extreme prejudice against the Sicilians, about whom he knew almost nothing except what he had learned from his parents. Once in another city, he refused to eat in a restaurant which had prepared an exceptional Italian meal for him at my behest because he perceived the owner to be Sicilian. As the philosopher Herbert Spencer wrote, "Contempt prior to investigation" has spoiled many lives and keeps one in ignorance.)

The influence upon Sicily by the Arabs, Greeks and Phoenicians (Lebanese) seems somewhat obvious, but this is the first book that I have read which researches the Arab relationship thoroughly and then presents recipes illustrating it.

It is not my purpose here to write a book review, but I found this one so interesting and some of the recipes so unusual that I think it is worthwhile to present a few here. I am assuming that the book is still in print. (I have written the publisher requesting permission to excerpt and assume its granting) and I recommend that you ask your bookstore to get it for you.

Here are some quite simple recipes from the book worth trying to get a taste of a different Sicily.

Fresh Lemon Salad
3 lemons, peeled and sliced thin
3 Tbls. extra-virgin olive oil
1/4 tsp. black pepper
Sea salt

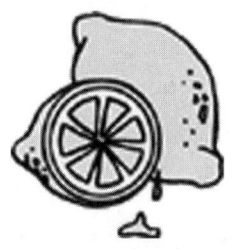

Arrange the lemon slices in a spiral on a plate. Pour the olive oil over, then sprinkle with pepper and a liberal amount of salt. Leave to marinate at room temperature for about an hour, then serve.

This is suggested as a refresher between courses instead of the current ubiquitous sorbet. He notes that this serves ten Americans or two Sicilians. I suggest that you will end up liking it. It does indeed refresh, and you should save the remainder of the olive oil/lemon/salt mixture and use as a sauce for the likes of cold beef, especially a piece of steak left over from the grill.

Orange Sauce
2 Tbls. unsalted butter
3 egg yolks
salt and pepper
2-1/2 Tbls. white wine vinegar
2 Tbls. orange juice (freshly squeezed)
grated zest (outer shell) of 1/2 an orange

Melt the butter in top half of double boiler. Remove from heat and add all the other ingredients. Return to the heat and start whisking constantly over medium heat. The sauce should thicken in about two or three minutes. Remove from heat at once and serve over steamed vegetables such as asparagus, beans, fennel, broccoli, etc.

In France this sauce is known as sauce maltaise. Now that you can get them in local stores, make this sauce with blood oranges for something really different.

Spaghetti with Fried Breadcrumbs & Raisins
1 clove of garlic peeled and crushed
1/4 C. olive oil
4 or 5 Tbls. of breadcrumbs
1/2 C. golden raisins
salt
1 lb. spaghetti
finely chopped Italian parsley
pepper

Lightly brown the garlic in the olive oil, but discard the garlic before it gets too brown or it will become bitter. Now saute the breadcrumbs in the olive oil, stirring constantly over medium heat for about two minutes. Soak the raisins in a bowl of warm water, not hot.

Cook the pasta al dente. Drain well. Drain the raisins after they plump. Toss the pasta, the raisins, the browned breadcrumbs, the parsley, salt and pepper. Be sure the spaghetti is well covered with breadcrumbs. Serve at once.

Chicken with Almonds
1 chicken, cut into eight pieces (3 to 3-1/2 pounds)
6 Tbls. olive oil
1 Tbls. tomato paste
4 Tbls. white wine vinegar
2 Tbls. sugar
1 tsp. salt
1/2 tsp. pepper
1/4 C. blanched almonds, crushed
1/4 C. blanched white almonds, toasted

Brown the chicken in two tablespoons of the olive oil over low heat; this will take about fifteen minutes. Drain the chicken and set aside.

Pour the remaining oil into the pan with the tomato paste dissolved in one cup of warm water. When the sauce begins to boil, add the vinegar, sugar, salt and pepper and the crushed almonds.

When the sauce returns to a boil, add the chicken pieces, lower the heat and cook, uncovered, for forty-five to fifty minutes, adding a little water if the sauce gets too thick. Turn the chicken pieces over at least once.

Arrange the chicken on a platter covered with some sauce. Sprinkle the toasted almonds on top. Serve warm in winter, room temperature in summer.

—July 1997

About manners, food, ruins and rejuvenation

The world has gotten loud, crude and rude to an embarrassing degree. The "finger" is replacing the eagle as a national symbol. Politicians in Washington insult the president while locally, autos race through the streets with sound systems blasting, forcing bystanders to listen to their music.

This culture degradation is often charged to TV, to male body piercing, long hair, baseball caps worn indoors, bill pointed to the rear, to rock and roll music (when I was young it was jazz that was bad for us, as well as Hemingway's sordid stories and James Joyce and Frank Harris, bootlegged into culture before "that Roosevelt Supreme Court" said it was okay to read about sex and all that kind of stuff).

In fact, I don't believe any of these factors have much to do with what's wrong. I think it's pretty silly to wear a cap indoors, and more silly yet to wear it backwards. I can't imagine piercing my ears or nose or lip or other unmentionable private parts to stick a hunk of metal in them. I wouldn't pay money to wear blue jeans with rips in them; I avoid as much as possible wearing articles of clothing with an outside advertisement on them. (Why would I want to spend money to advertise someone's product; this is the biggest most successful advertising scam yet perpetuated upon America's citizenry.) Still, for the life of me, I can't connect the silliness of the above actions as being the *cause* of unmannerliness. While there is a certain amount of plain *training* involved in learning good manners, I believe the real cause of inconsideration is the result of an absence of awe, a failure to see and feel the mystery beyond the material. Those people we might dismiss or be rude to are not just bodies intruding on our space, but live humans, each a story, a collection of life experiences of which are just as great, just as painful to them as ours are to us. Nobody comes into the world without help and no one leaves with his hearse followed by a U-Haul full of possessions. Friends and Islands of Politeness, Grace and Gentleness are all we leave behind. And, all we take with us.

We just returned from a trip to Seattle (a remarkably polite city, by the way) and while I was there I read about the Jane Austen Society of North America and its sister organization, the Polite Society. Austen is the author of *Sense and Sensibility* and *Pride and Prejudice,* writings full of wit and outstanding characterizations, in a period of costume and ceremony.

The Polite Society reportedly exacts a Politeness Pledge, swearing to practice unremitting courtesy to family, friends, associates, tradespeople and shop assistants, bar and restaurant staff and other road users.

So, no matter which direction your cap's bill points or how many earrings you wear, or whether you have elegant rips in your jean, or if you dress from the Gazebo or Brooks Bros. I would suggest (with great courtesy and respect) that taking the Politeness Pledge could add a wonderful dimension to all our lives.

• • •

More Seattle interest:
I'm not sure if anyone in Seattle drinks martinis or beer or Scotch, but the whole area is awash in espresso, cappuccino, latte and cof-

fee Americano. The *New York Times* reports that outside Seattle at a Texaco station on Highway 167, a huge banner facing the road offers regular commuters "Free espresso with six fill-ups." Nearby, a smaller banner says "cleans vital engine parts."

From the same paper is the story of an invasion force heading our way. McDonalds and 7-Eleven are both pushing espresso and cappuccino and their armies of tiny styrofoam cups are moving east. I suppose it was inevitable. Someone always can take a great product, mass produce it and destroy the qualities that made it popular in the first place. Remember when there were real hamburgers and cheeseburgers around?

• • •

I want to pass along to you two paragraphs of my favorite resume of 1994, possibly of forever, just as I received it.
Sir/Madam,

I am currently working towards a degree at Northern Michigan University. Whilst in pursuit of this goal it has come to my attention that your business has an employment position open.

I find that your position available, within a median of 20 hours per week, is congruent with my needs as a continuing student for this summer and for the following school year here in Marquette.

No comment by me is required.

• • •

Preservation of the ruins
Nineteen-ninety-four has run out, but the stamina of the old Heritage House, the Rosewood Inn and the ugly black and rusting ore dock approach is amazing. If you missed the letter to the editor in *The Mining Journal* on Sunday, December 18 by Kenneth Hogg you missed a gem. He puts it better than I'm likely to, so find a copy and save it—it's a treasure.

• • •

Care and growth of the living

Despite the above lament, almost everything is very well in downtown Marquette:

- Once again, the holiday lighting was beautiful as were all of the decorations. (The Scrooge in me says that the "Santa House" in the pocket park is out of tune with the rest of the city's decoration quality. I sort of expect Santa to say "woof" when someone walks past.)
- The new (certainly it was more than mere remodeling) First National Bank building on Washington Street and its elegant interior bring much class to downtown. A truly beautiful addition. How banking has changed!
- The new Delft Theatre entrance location on Main Street, and the elimination of the bowling lanes building there have incorporated Main Street into the downtown mainstream. Now it is a part of Center City, not just a street to drive through, going somewhere else.
- The remodeling and restyling of the Detroit and Northern building lobby is just beautifully done in mahogany and light blue/gray. It's worth a visit.
- Not far from D&N, the Marquette Mall is coming back to life with several new stores opening.
- And on South Third Street just past the fire hall, the old ungainly former Catholic Credit Union building is no longer ungainly, but is alive and healthy with the Elder Agency as its new owner. This inside renovation is very fine and plans for the outside in the spring will make this once plain building a worthy addition to downtown.

I'm sure that the loss of the air base people will have an effect on us, but growth seems to be the activity most noticeable now.

● ● ●

Suicide walk?

The intersection of Genesee Street and South Front Street (US 41/M 28) presents several very serious problems, I think.

Witness: There is a pedestrian walk signal controlling the walk across South Front, a distance from curb to curb of about sixty feet.

Stirring It Up!

The walk signal is on white for eight seconds, then one might continue walking for the twelve seconds remaining of the vehicle green signal and if one wanted to live dangerously, could continue for the approximate five-second caution. But the safe walk signal is eight seconds. To make it across in eight seconds, one needs to go into serious running training because crossing that highway in that time period is equivalent to running a six- to seven-minute mile, which few of us have done recently.

In addition: When a Blondeau lime truck takes advantage of the amber light to start a left turn onto Genesee off South Front, it blocks the Genesee traffic's left turn on its proper green time, which is only twenty seconds to begin with. These trucks are long, slow and cumbersome and they chew up a hunk of safe green time. I have seen some serious near-misses at this corner. There seems to be no fault here, only traffic engineering needing some serious thought. I sure as heck can't think of a cure, but someone smarter in these matters ought to be able to modify things a bit.

—January 1995

The Politeness Pledge

So far as it is in my power I will at all times be courteous to those with whom I have personal dealings. I accept that this includes:

- members of my family
- those whom I consult professionally
- other road users
- tradesmen and shop assistants
- bar and restaurant staff

As a member of the Polite Society I will exercise the maximum self-control in all situations likely to test my patience and temper.

At the start of each day I will make a resolution to deal with every situation as I meet it with the utmost consideration for other people's feelings.

I will be especially conscious of the need to be courteous to people whose style of life may differ from my own.

I will (if male) treat women with an especial courtesy, observing habits of chivalry towards them. I will abstain from conduct or language likely to cause embarrassment or offense to those in whose company I am at any time.

It was a pretty slow millenium, but a damn fast century

There is a terrible tendency as the clocks tick away toward the end of both a Century and a Millenium to use such historic markers to review the Past and to write ponderous pieces (it won't happen here) dripping with significance. An immediate problem crops up, however, as clocks don't "tick" any more. I know of pseudo-Grandfather clocks leaning against walls which not only don't "tick" but which do not "tock" either. How is one to know the Time?

I have a Hamilton railroad pocket watch, gold-encased which belonged to my father. It requires winding and it ticks away the flight of Time. My father knew all about time. His watch not only ticked and tocked, friendly, reassuring sounds when one holds the watch to the ear, but it required care; its driving spring had to be wound each day, preferably at a specified time, morning or evening usually. It was required for his job as a railroad engineer that once each month the watch be taken to a jeweler designated by the railroad for a time check. The jeweler's clock was the local standard and it measured the only time worth bothering about. I wear an L.

L. Bean Hamilton wrist watch which never says anything to me as its silent hands mark the passing of my life. It's a poor companion. I hold it to my ear and there is no tick and no tock and unlike an empty conch shell, I do not even hear the surf, pounding, far away.

Proving my knowledge of events from the late 1920s to the present is not difficult. I am living it. Before my personal memories start I can select from stories told to me, sometimes reinforced with contemporary evidence. In this way my memories extend for the full Century.

My father was eleven when the new century came to Calumet, a real town, almost a city in those days. There were churches everywhere, one for each foreign influx—Finns, Croatians, Slovenians, French, Italians, English, Norwegians, Swedes. The Calumet Theatre already was busy with famous visitors, especially opera singers, throwing their arias into the cold streets. The wide, boulevard-like Sixth Street, not yet host to what is now arguably the region's ugliest shopping center, was full of people, wagons drawn by mules and by horses. My father's father was a drayman, an almost professional sounding term for someone who drove a wagon pulled by horses. Are there any draymen left? And, of course, there were bars to serve all the ethnic groups; an Italian relative opened the bar next door to the theatre, now known as Shute's, then known as Curto's.

Six years into the new century at age sixteen my father went to work, progressing from a blacksmith's helper to a sandman's helper, a hostler's helper and then a fireman on the Mineral Range RR in Calumet. With the promise of better pay, a better job on a larger railroad he moved to Marquette in 1912. And, though I was not born, of course, this move is fixed in my modern memory this way: in the middle 1980s I was in a checkout line at a local grocery store and in the adjacent line an elderly, slim man said "Are you Charlie Curto's boy?" Even though I thought the "boy" part was inaccurate, I asked how he knew me? "You look like your dad and I helped him move into his room on Bluff Street in 1912." My father's first room in town was in a house on the North side of Bluff

Stirring It Up!

Street, just off of Third. The questioner was John Herron who had been a "Call Boy" for the D.S.S. & A. RR and who lived into his middle 90s, spry and firm of memory. Call Boys were men who did exactly what the title sounds like—they called workers by going to their homes or rooms and getting them out of bed to notify them of work times. Few people had telephones. I can remember when the Call Boy would wake my dad for an early run by pounding on the front door. Sometimes this would be 3:00 a.m. My memory of these calls is that it was always winter which meant that my father had a very long, cold walk to the roundhouse at the end of Spring Street. If he had enough time he might prepare a big breakfast for both of us. Pork chops, potatoes, eggs and toast, which might have to last him until he got to St. Ignace and transferred his train to the big ferry and to the care of the New York Central RR. Then it was his habit to cook a meal in the roundhouse for the train crew. I usually went back to bed after a meal of this size and somehow woke in time for school or if there were lights on at my grandmother Tobin's house next door, I went there to spend time with her. This is the Irish-French (and Indian) side of my family and there are many tales there, too, for another day.

On Christmas Day of 1913 my father rode the train home to Calumet, to face the death of his younger sister. The "Italian Hall Tragedy" had taken place on Christmas Eve of 1913. The Italian Hall, now torn down, was the Societa Mutua Beneficenza Italiana or the Italian Mutual Benefit Society. Poor pay and dangerous working conditions had brought the Western Federation of Miners (WFM) into the area in 1908. Negotiations for forming a union broke down and a general strike was called on July 23, 1913 idling over 15,000 working in the area. Violence erupted early and no settlement headway had been made by the Christmas season. National Guardsmen had been sent in by Governor Ferris and Clarence Darrow, the famous Chicago attorney, who represented the union was reportedly negotiating with the governor to end the strike.

Members of the union organized a Christmas party for the children of union members in the ballroom of the Italian Hall, which was on the second floor. About 700 children and parents attended. In the midst of the festivities, a "dark haired man shouted loudly above the din of joy, FIRE, FIRE, SEE SEE FIRE!" motioning people to head for the stairway exit. The double doors at the bottom of the stairwell only opened inward and the pileup of bodies prevented that. Seventy-three persons died there. Thirty-two thousand persons marched in a cold, snowy funeral procession.

It was called the Italian Hall Tragedy, but in fact of the seventy-three adults and children killed, the official death list proclaims that there were forty-nine Finns, fourteen Croatians, six Slovenians, one Swede and only three Italians. Of those three, my father's younger sister, Katarina Bronzo, was one. She was only twenty-one years old, married to Peter Bronzo and carried in her arms an infant daughter, Renee, as I knew her much later. When my aunt was crushed at the bottom of the stairs the family story says, she held the child over her head and someone saved her.

Another of my father's sisters, Mae, took Katarina's place as the wife of Peter Bronzo. After Pete and Mae moved to Flint they had a small farm with a few cows, a large garden and a big house. He invested in land in Flint and this paid off in later years when Renee leased land to commercial interests rather than selling it, becoming, reportedly, quite well to do.

Visits to Pete and Mae Bronzo were exciting vacations. The Curtos had become tightly tied to the Bronzos. My dad's younger sister, Ann, had married Tony, Pete's younger brother. Tony operated a restaurant just outside the main gate to the Buick plant and I recall visiting there when the fledgling UAW strike against Buick was on. I think that Tony's place was a hangout for the strikers, because I recall some conversations and the place was crowded with picketers. Ann and Tony had a daughter, Gloria.

My cousin Gloria was my age and we milked the two cows, side by side at Pete's farm on the other side of town. Sometimes we exhibited a childish romantic relationship by squirting milk on each other. Sunday morning special coffee was made of fresh milk from their cows, strong black coffee, eggs whipped into the hot mixture

Stirring It Up!

and a liberal amount of red wine. The froth was worth the work. Each year, Pete, his brother Tony and some other Italians in the area imported a railway car of grapes from Californaia and made their own wine. Children were not allowed the strong drink with wine, but we managed to sneak some. I had a twelve-year old's crush on my cousin. (Years later when she went to Michigan State and I went to the University of Michigan I sometimes hitch-hiked from Ann Arbor to East Lansing to date her. She was beautiful.)

Don enjoys life in the 20th century

Every family has historical events dotting the family lifeline extending usually from grandparents to whatever time the present is. Sometimes the events that seem to be remembered by everyone through all the generations are tragedies, or sometimes the event seems just plain silly.

A near tragedy in my family was the almost-death of my mother in the 1918 flu pandcmic. Apparently Marquette was hit hard by the "flu bug" as we once called the virus. (My uncle John escaped the flu by being taken out of school.) My mother seemed to flirt with danger, as another well-remembered story about Ruth Tobin is the time when she and some friends went from house to house, retrieving from the mailboxes the then-permitted samples of ExLax that had been placed there as advertising. After all, it tasted like chocolate. One can only imagine the results.

A family connection to a historic event revolves around World War I and Picnic Rocks in Marquette. This area was turned into a training camp for Michigan soldiers slated to go to Europe. If I follow the events correctly as sketched in a photo album put together by my mother there was a young soldier training there who was romantically involved with her. He had an Irish name and he was killed in Europe just a month before the war ended, a bit more than eighty-one years ago, not long as the crow flies. I don't recall this relationship being talked about ever either by my mother or by her parents, but in my remembered families, not much of a personal nature was ever talked about in the presence of children. I'm not sure that the adults talked about personal matters, either. In fact, I'm guessing that if anybody had sex in those faraway days, it was in total blackness. I know that I was "found under a cabbage leaf" as my mother said. I found this comforting in my pre-adolescent years because there was a period when I couldn't imagine being related to anyone I was living with. In later years, I realized that I was issued by the U.S. Marine Corps.

Apparently cabbage became a real bumper crop because in 1923 the population of the world was not yet two billion and last month the world population topped six billion. There are very few ills in the world that in one way or another aren't related to over-population. It is clear that people everywhere must stop having sex for a while, even in dark rooms.

A wonderfully pleasant memory in a paricularly terrible time in this century is the 1935 World Series. I don't know how my father managed to pull it off—for 1935 was a Depression Year and money was scarce and my father just had returned to work on the railroad after being out of work for "two years and eleven months" (a Depression mantra marking his worst personal depression when he walked the floors at night, unable to sleep, worrying, lamenting his lot, desperate to put food on the table for us, a feat that he managed with the willingness to take any job and considerable help from my mostly ungracious French and Irish grandparents toward an "Italian." Those were mostly bad days. Whoever said, if anyone did, that poverty and hardship develop strength of character was an idiot. Poverty and hardship bring on selfishness, meaness, secretiveness, prejudice and war)—but, suddenly there we were, just he and I staying with his brother Tom in Detroit with tickets to watch Mickey Cochrane manage the Detroit Tigers to victory in the World Series. They beat Charley Grimm's Chicago Cubs. My uncle Tom had a Chevrolet and we rode to the stadium in style. It was pretty heady stuff for a kid from Marquette. My father loved baseball and so did I in the days when players stayed with the "home team" for most of their careers and if Hank Greenberg was a Tiger this year, chances were pretty good that he'd be one next year, too. I know all about the player "slavery" of those old days, but for the baseball fan it was better than watching a bunch of over-paid prima donnas with no team attachment beyond the treasurer's office. In later years I saw the Brooklyn Dodgers play when I lived in New York and watched Jackie Robinson. I knew then that I was watching history, but nothing else ever has seemed as exciting as the 1935 World Series.

Along came World War II, just in time to select an immediate career choice for most of us. It seems to me that everyone I knew did what war service was required. I did not know then, nor do I know now anyone who was a "slacker" or who tried mightily to avoid military service. Some of us were in college and we were selected for the V-12 program not because we were exceptional but merely because we were in the right place at the right time and we fell into someone's quota. For many of us this was the gift of life because it increased survival chances. I enlisted in the Marine Corps, something I like to think that I would do again, under similar circumstances. If you didn't know your capacity for accepting torture and humiliation, some time in the Corps living through Parris Island and Quantico would teach you. Not everyone was able to deal with the often degrading treatment the military felt necessary to our future edification. Some just dropped out via the medical discharge system. There always was suicide, which was used sometimes. Most of us just refused to let the bastards win. Over the years I have revised my definition of a successful Marine: if you did all the jobs it asked of you without trying to avoid them and you are breathing today, you are successful.

In order to be successful completely, however, one must remember instantly, without having to look up written record, what his serial numbers were, or perhaps are, since one never ceases in a part of him to be a Marine. Enlisted number 532678; officer number 045747. I have forgot my boot camp rifle number but my DI was killed late in the war, so it doesn't matter any more anyway. Besides, that was in another time, on a small Pacific Island.

There is a long list of things in the last half of this century that I don't like, but I'm not going to bother you with them because you have your long own list of things you don't like and they are much more important than those on my list. So, let's leave it at that for the time being. There's plenty of time in the new century; or at least it seems that way, now. Talk to you in the next Century, along about the year 2000.

—December 1999

Stirring It Up!

On being an American citizen
"Nullius addictus jurare in verba magister" *

* - Horace: "I am not bound to swear allegiance to the dogmas of any master."

Winter, 1945, China

In 1945 I was a young, inexperienced Marine second lieutenant on the tropical island of Guam. In autumn of that year we set sail over stormy seas for North China's Tientsin. The weather in this once heavily industrialized city was a never-finished jigsaw puzzle of heavy clouds, once-in-awhile pallid sun, mean temperatures, rain, violent winds, sand storms and bitter, damp loneliness. Thanksgiving and Christmas were around a faraway corner. No two holidays seemed to me more unnatural living in that desolate, poverty-wracked land. It is important to this piece that the reader understands the huge cultural separation one experienced in China at that time...from the familiar, from home, from America. The Chinese tolerated us, barely; the Nationalists because they were doomed without us and the Communists because they were betting on the Nationalists' doom. The Japanese we were there to "repatriate" were frightened that we might abandon our protection and let the Chinese at them. Except for contrary orders, many gladly would have done that. We sent women and children back to Japan packed like upright sardines in LSTs which bounced their way across the shallow Yellow Sea. It wasn't a very pleasant job then or in present reflection. But at the end of WWII the Japanese were not a very appealing people.

The White Russian former backers of the Russian Czar and some of the longtime German outcasts who lived in cultural isolation among the Chinese and mostly were despised welcomed us, the males with hands out but also with fear, the women, especially the young women with complete and hungry abandon knowing that they stood the best chance of extracting food and maybe some semblance of romance beyond sex, and finally, protection from the Chinese.

It was in this setting of turmoil and loneliness that one day as I listened to North China Marine Radio "America the Beautiful" was broadcast. I remember as though it was yesterday. A strong sense of loneliness came over me. Tears came to my eyes. The impact was powerful and emotions cascaded over me. This was more than simple patriotism or loneliness or homesickness. It was a kind of epiphany (a word usually associated with more godly feelings but it seems to fit here), an instant understanding and powerful awareness of how fortunate, how lucky I was to be an American. (I almost want to put the word "blessed" in here but I worry the implication.) I had many times before in service felt a wonderful emotional warmth but this was different and deeper and the recollection of the feeling persists in strength to this day. Somewhere at the core of my person, I understood that no one could be luckier. Being an American citizen then was luck of the highest order. It still is. When I note the power of being an American citizen then (and now) I am not speaking of the "ugly American" syndrome wherein everything he surveys is his and all is inferior to what is at home. Rather, one felt gratitude, security, pride, power. This is how I have lived in America from that time to this time. Travels in foreign countries were exciting but always were better because beneath current enjoyment was the knowledge (often not thought of) that I was American, that my base was solid, secure, respected.

That was then.

• • •

Now 2002 here

I really am not sure whether the United States is the greatest country that ever existed, but I cannot think of one that has published a document like our Declaration of Independence. I am aware that this document does not have legal force, but it eloquently spells out both the beliefs and the goals of the new country. Where else do you read that all of us have a right to pursue Happiness (with a capital H)? That we all are equal? It declares that liberty is a right and that we are to be free of government tyranny in our everyday lives. To this day, some are more equal than others, but great strides toward political equality have been made in my lifetime and more are needed.

We are in a period of great change. Terrorism is driving us down different, dark paths where citizens now accept new rights restraints. As government officials, elected and appointed, assume ever greater powers over our lives, I am reminded of Lord Acton's statement (in a letter in 1887): "Power tends to corrupt and absolute power corrupts absolutely." It needs to be a daily safety reminder to cause us to be especially observant of changes, for even at the lowest level of authority, a governmental position has power. This dictum is known well and often attention and emphasis is placed mostly on the last half: absolute power corrupts absolutely. I think more thought needs to be given to the beginning observation, "power tends to corrupt..." If this is true, then careful observation needs to begin with the lowest position in government or in business. There is a corollary to Acton's that is perturbing: the belief that he who has power acquires wisdom with it. The man credited with major composition of the Declaration of Independence, Thomas Jefferson, had a solid feel for the dangers of power when he wrote, "an honest man can feel no pleasure in the exercise of power over his fellow citizens." Well!

Remembering the great sense of gratitude I had in China in that long ago year for being an American citizen requires that I also remember that my fellow citizens who occupy offices which have power over me do so with my permission (and yours) and not because of their personal brilliance. Occupying the office does not make the person any smarter than before he occupied the office. It is the small misuse of power, the tiny corruption, an office holder's disdain for a person, that needs constant watching.

There are so many examples of the truth of Lord Acton's statement it needs no detailed defense. The tortured career of Richard Nixon can be explained in part by it.

Many years ago, I was in a long line at a bank in Delaware and heard a commotion at the teller window ahead of me. I heard the teller, a man, say, "I don't make those kinds of mistakes." My attention was caught by that arrogant remark and the elderly man in front of the teller said, nicely I thought, "you didn't count the money right." Another strong denial of error from the teller and the elderly man left the line and as he passed those of us standing there said, "Well, I was going to give him his twenty dollars back, but to Hell with him." It is clear that the position of power made the teller smarter.

Top U.S. government officials from time to time recently have made what sound like doomsday pronouncements regarding imminent terror strikes for which they do not offer us supporting details. The "alerts" tell us to be alert. Possible, seemingly logical targets are discussed and then the press gets in the act and tells us how to knock out a target or two. This tends to keep the populace in a constant state of frenzy. People in frenzy and fear are a people who can be controlled more easily. This is the administration that confidently set out to capture or kill Osama bin Laden and his top people. The former targets still frighten the hunters. Is there no one else who is worried about President Bush's pronouncement of our being in a permanent, unending war? (Recently President Bush referred to his administration as "his government." It is our government.

Stirring It Up!

This is not a distinction to be tossed lightly about.)

These also are the same people who ignore, at least publicly, Hamas and other terrorist organizations in the Middle East as though they were only there to attack Israel and have no real meaning to us. What happened to President Bush's pronouncement to the effect that "if you harbor terrorists" you are terrorists? These also are the same people who ignore, at least publicly, the involvement of Saudi Arabia with the terrorists, using our need for oil as a largely unspoken reason. Oil in the ground does not bring wealth to Saudi Arabia so the Saudis need our cooperation before that oil becomes money.

We either are a great power, period, or we are a great power when some of our suppliers permit us to be one.

And what has happened to the once great opposition party liberals? Where have they gone? Is everyone afraid to talk about the emperor's costume? Where are the opposition views on the handling of Enron corruption, the spreading corruption in the top corporations, the remaking of the stock market into a giant casino? Does anyone think that the almost daily ups and downs of the market have anything to do with the real value of the companies whose stocks bound around?

Isn't there anyone disturbed about the docility with which air travel passengers accept disgusting personal intrusions; many of which, taken at face value, are plain nonsense. Every covert test of airline security has showed how permeable the system is. Now the government plans to hire 57,500 security personnel.

Our democracy still can be saved, but a "permanent war," a national state of frenzy for a generation, could so alter the populace that no one but old people like I have become will even know what an American democracy is or was.

Frightening, isn't it?

So be skeptical of the righteous public servant, question political piety, watch for travelers with bulky jackets, thick heeled shoes, shifty eyes, and sullen attitudes on sunny days.

—July 2002

The greatest generations

It must have been 1954 when former President Harry S Truman stopped in Wilmington, Delaware on his way to New York. The Executive Committee of the Democratic Party had arranged a short reception in the DuPont Hotel. I was the editor of a local newspaper and also was doing some party publicity work so I was invited. There probably were about thirty-five people there and after we all were introduced to him, Truman joined small groups talking about the fall campaigns. I watched for an opportunity to talk with him. I wished to thank him for ordering the drop of the atomic bomb on Japan. This event, as terrible as some might view it now, probably saved my life and in those days, I was grateful for such small favors.

I was in the Third Marine Division on Guam after the war was ended and we learned that the area that had been selected for our landing on Japan's home islands was said to be defended by twenty-two Home Guard divisions. Marines are good, and many of us in our youth considered ourselves immortal, but later reflection made me believe that we all would have been slaughtered on those beaches by people defending their homes.

I managed to get close to him and re-introduced myself. He asked what I was doing for the party. I told him and he said, "Work hard. That's important work." He had a way of drawing one to him. So, I plunged into an area where I suspected later that I didn't really belong and thanked him. He looked intently at me and I thought that perhaps a presidential reprimand was coming. He said after a minute "a man has to do what he has to do." He turned away, to more pleasant talk.

The point of this story at this time?

I think that "the greatest generation" idea is better for selling books than for properly defining one generation relative to others. It's comfortable to be a member of that generation, but I would give up the comfort for about fifty years less age. Men and women do what has to be done when confronted.

Not to push the thought too far, but would any of us consider the firemen and policemen in the New York disaster to be of a lesser generation than "the greatest generation?" They did "what they had to do." The much maligned younger generations have not had anything to do. So, why would a person do what he has to do when there is nothing that he has to do?

Stand by for a new "greatest generation." Or two.

—October 2001

At the end, a lethal injection

We had the patient on the examining table; she was frightened at first. We held her, wrapped in our arms. The tremors slowed, disappeared. Soon she was calm, resting. The doctor carefully shaved the hair from the shin part of her left leg, then she tied a rubber tourniquet just above the patient's knee, tightened it to bring an artery into relief which she rubbed with an alcohol swab.

As the doctor inserted the needle into the leg, the patient looked at her, then at us and she seemed to know then that this was no ordinary needle. A slight shudder went though her and what rigidity there had been relaxed. The drugs put her to sleep, just like the kind of sleep that I had seen before, a gentle, relaxed sleep. The rest of the liquid in the large needle continued to be injected and the sleep deepened, the patient slumped, the patient's heart stopped; the patient was dead. This is what a lethal injection is like.

The patient was our Black Labrador of thirteen years, Kate.

Death may be less than nothing as Edna St. Vincent Millay said, but it is quiet and it is final. Once, many years ago, with a stethescope listening for the last heartbeat of a loved one, I heard life go away. One doesn't hear the beginning of death, just the end of life. It is instantaneous, there is no delay. The heart stops. Life is gone. The body is there. But the spirit is gone. That strange, not understood force leaves. That's what happens. But it is more than that, too. A person, a dog, is not just an arrangement of organs and functions but a connection, a part of the web of our life.

Katharine Hepburn Tikkanen-Curto

With death, a hole is ripped in this fabric. It takes a long time to weave new life to fill the tear. Death is very quiet, making no announcement of its intentions. I don't think that death is a friend.

In death Kate looks like...Kate. Her head rests between her outstreched paws, as though she were just asleep, a favorite position. In life, at home, alive, her eyes looked up at me. They are motionless now. We say goodbye to Kate, our first goodbye in death with just a beginning realization of how barren we are to be in the near future as we face the loss of such a family member. For many days and nights now everywhere I turn at home I will see Kate. Her bark to go out early in the morning has wakened me; but she is not there. That spirit is somewhere. Can a spirit bark? Manifest itself alongside the sofa, under the dining table, in the kitchen, waiting at the door? Can a spirit put its cold nose against my hand to wake me from a nap?

I know that when one writes about a Black Labrador friend who has died there is the requirement often performed by other writers to tell a heroic story of a great dog. I am not sure that Kate was a "great dog," but she was my dog and I loved her; in fact Kate was probably lucky to have lived to just four days shy of 13 years.

Kate was known formally to the American Kennel Club as Katharine Hepburn Tikkanen-Curto, so named because of her irrepressible love of life and her total immunity to any kind of punishment life might throw at her. Kate was the product of one of the best Labrador kennels in America, Shamrock Acres operated by Sally McCarthy in Madison, Wisconsin.

I previously had had a Black Lab from Sally's shop, Sgt. Pepper, and sought another similar personality after Sgt. Pepper died in 1986. We wanted a female this time, mostly because when they squat to pee, it is a one-time affair, none of this running around the area, lifting a leg ten times. When we got to the kennel in early August of 1988 there were three female pups remaining from the litter. Sally brought them out to the lawn, in the sunlight, and let all three out. As the Chinese often say, all Caucasians look alike, and the three puppies were alike as triplets. We could not choose. Finally I decided that we should take the first one to squat, thus we would begin the return trip to Marquette under dry circumstances. Her independence cropped up early; she was comfortable on the back seat of the car, without a lot of holding and petting. She eyed us a little suspiciously but there were no slips on the trip home.

I do not have allowed space nor the words to narrate details about Kate's first year. Given only a few words, I guess the first year, controlled by Kate, could be labeled accurately as Terror and Destruction. We lived in terror of what destruction was being planned by her. Kate was out of the same family line as Sgt. Pepper, but somehow, the easy-to-train-and-domesticate gene got lost in previous generations. It was Kate's idea that we needed training, she was fine.

Almost daily I said I would give her one more day, then it was execution; friends who saw what a difficult dog she was agreed with me. I almost was ready to put her out for adoption when I found Bob Olson at River Road Kennel just out of Lena, Wisconsin. We made a deal over the phone; I gave him adequate warning about her. She was with him for three months. I visited a number of times for training, too. On one visit I asked him why she was as she was? "Well," he said, "nothing on earth happens fast enough for Kate." Of course; I understood. Had she been a human, Ritalin would have been prescribed. During retrieving training Kate left the mark so fast that it appeared that she was trying to walk on the top of the water. Real training began after she tired a little. I am not a serious hunter of waterfowl, but Kate did become a very good retriever and as we live next to a pond, she got plenty of practice. After the three month period (and the dollars that went with it) both Kate and I were trained, but neither of us was perfect. Clearly, Kate owed her long, good life to the initial work of Bob Olson.

I spent a lot of the next two years training Kate and she training me. Gradually we came to an understanding: she would perform most of the social behaviors that I sought if I didn't try to compromise her basic independence. This was, in our relationship, a kind of mutual wariness; it was sort of an animal/human Mutual Asssured Destruction program, as each of us had the ability to destroy the other. Kate was not a barker and she was beloved of the kennel keepers, especially Rita at the Animal Inn, which we referred to as "the resort." She was, as is expected of Labradors, friendly to almost all other dogs (except those small, fluffy, noisy, yapping creatures) and to most people, except those whom she sensed were not truly dog lovers, who did not consider dogs equal or superior to humans. (Let's digress a second or two on the issue of superiority. Only inferior people need to prove superiority; if one is superior, the comfort is in the knowing, not in the proving.) Kate could sleep through loud noise, she could walk out of the house without boots in January when the outside temperature was zero, she never asked where we were going, if we were going that was enough. She was not a complainer. Kate never asked for much from us; she knew exactly who was superior and she enjoyed her position.

Over the years Kate tended toward vegetarianism. The dried dog food was okay; some chicken was okay, too. The special diet that her doc put her on in later life worked well to get weight off, but the really great stuff consisted of bananas, orange segments (especially Clementines), grapes of both hues, apples, especially those in the fields that had fallen from trees and rotted just a little, and for field tasting nothing beat rose hips nipped off the bush. Kate joined me for several blueberry picking expeditions but I had to discontinue that because she would strip the plants completely, leaves, small twigs and all the berries whether ripe or not.

Kate's most famous adventure came one afternoon in late autumn when Pat and she were walking a trail which went to the base of Marquette mountain, then veered east toward the south edge of Shiras Hills. This is a moderately wooded area with some rocky small rises along the way. It is one of a number of favorite walks that they had taken many times before. On this day, as it got near sunset, Pat slipped on some mossy rocks, and with legs in the air, she twisted and heard a snap, and she knew her leg was broken.

When she didn't return after an hour on the walk I got worried and as I didn't know which trail they had taken, my search was fruitless. After an hour and a half I called 911 and eventually Search and Rescue came to my home, got organized and took off looking for them. However, they never did find them until Pat and Kate "rescued themselves" in the backyard of a home at the very edge of Shiras Hills. The home's owner had phoned 911 when this strange crawling woman, with a black dog, appeared in his yard just past sunset. By the time I got there, there was an ambulance, several police cars, plus quite a few Search and Rescue people. After I took Kate home, first getting her out of her protective mode, I went to the emergency room to meet Pat. Then I got the story.

No one else came on the trail after Pat fell. No one heard her calls. There was no place to send Kate for help. Pat could not walk so she crawled, stopped, rested, crawled some more, for over two hours. Kate stayed close to her all the way, and as Pat puts it, she and Kate sang 4-H songs from Pat's youth to keep their spirits up. As time passed, Pat's leg began to throb and there was no sign of rescuers; by then it was almost dark and getting cold. Pat credits Kate's close and warm company with making that two hour crawl bearable. At home that night, after Pat came from the hospital, Kate appeared to rest but regularly looked at Pat, as though making sure that she was being cared for properly.

That's the kind of Black Labrador Kate was. From puppy days she kept a sharp eye on the world. Now she is dead and the tear in the fabric of my life is huge and ragged and only blackness shows through. The hole will get mended, but an important mark will remain. I learned a lot about me from that dog. We started as opponents. We ended in love.

Note: Dr. Kellie Holmstrom and the Clinic staff have made a contribution in Kate's name to the Michigan State University Veterinary School. Kate always appreciated Class.

—July 2001

Recipe Index

Asparagus, 29, 31
   Flamande, 51
   with eggs, 31
   with pasta, 31

Bolognese meat sauce, 183

Bread, 38, 61, 79

Broccoli, braised Romana, 52

Brussels sprouts, 51
   Braised, in cream, 190
   Italiana, 52

Cake
   Chocolate cream, 81
   Terry's chocolate, 94

Cheerios, toasted, 89

Chicken
   with almonds, 205
   Braised with vegetables, 192
   Broth, 66
   Italian roast, 28
   with tarragon, 71

Cornish hens with sesame, 192

Fish, lemon balm steamed, 71

Herb salad, 72

Lamb shanks with beans, 163

Lamprey, 107

Lemon salad, 203

Meat & beans, 92

Orange sauce, 204

Pasta, mystery, 72

Pesto, 73

Risotto with raisins, 186

Soup
    Bread & broth, 65
    Confetti vegetable, 67
    Cucumber dill, 193
    Onion & bread, 65
    Royal, 93
    Ten-curve bean, 67
    Zucchini, 79

Spaghetti with breadcrumbs & raisins, 204

Tomato Sandwiches, 105

Venison chili with apples, 191